THE BIBLE SERIES

WHAT
EVERYONE
NEEDS TO KNOW ABOUT THE
BIBLE

DON STEWART

What Everyone Needs To Know About The Bible

© 2016 By Don Stewart

Published by EOW (Educating Our World)
San Dimas, California 91773
All rights reserved
www.educatingourworld.com

TABLE OF CONTENTS

INTRODUCTION

The grass withers, the flower fades but the word of our God will stand forever (Isaiah 40:8 ESV).

Jesus said: Heaven and earth will pass away, but my words will not pass away (Matthew 24:35 KJV).

The Christian faith is based upon a Book—the Bible. In this volume we will look at some introductory questions concerning this "Book of Books." These include: What kind of book is the Bible? What does it claim for itself? Why is it so important to study this one book? "Why does humanity need a written revelation from God?" If the Bible claims to be the Word of God, then why should we believe it?

These questions are primary. Indeed, they must be answered before any serious study of the Bible can begin.

What Is
the Bible?

So, what is the Bible?

The English word Bible simply means "book." It is derived from the Latin word *biblia* and the Greek words *biblion* and *biblos* meaning, "scroll" or "book." While the word Bible may simply mean book, to Christians, it has a much greater and deeper meaning.

THE BIBLE IS THE SACRED SCRIPTURE OF CHRISTIANS

Christians use the term *Bible* to refer to the sixty-six books that they hold to be sacred Scripture. The Bible, however, is not simply a collection of holy books, it is *one* Book—one continuous unfolding story from beginning to end. Indeed, it is the account of the living God revealing Himself, as well as His eternal plan, to the human race.

IT IS THE FINAL AUTHORITY ON EVERYTHING IT DEALS WITH

The term "Bible" also has the idea of preeminence—it is the final authority on all matters of faith and practice. The Bible, therefore, is not merely one of many books that have been written—it is *the Book*!

Consider the following testimonies to the Bible. . .

> England has two books, the Bible and Shakespeare. England made Shakespeare, but the Bible made England. (Victor Hugo)

> I believe the Bible is the best gift God has ever given to man. All the good from the Savior of the world is communicated to us through this book. (Abraham Lincoln)

> The New Testament is the very best book that ever was or ever will be known in the world. (Charles Dickens)

When the English poet Sir Walter Scott was on his deathbed he said to his biographer John Lockhart, "Bring me the Book." Lockhart inquired, "Which book?" Scott replied, "There is but one BOOK." Sir Walter Scott then passed away with his hand on the Bible.

Thus, the Bible is recognized as being in a class by itself. It is the only Book ever written that reveals God's Word to humanity.

FIVE IMPORTANT OBSERVATIONS ABOUT THE BIBLE

This being the case, it is necessary to make a number of preliminary observations about the Bible. They include the following.

OBSERVATION 1: THE BIBLE IS MADE UP OF TWO MAIN SECTIONS: THE OLD TESTAMENT AND THE NEW TESTAMENT

The Bible is made up of two testaments—the Old and the New. The Old Testament is about three times larger than the New Testament. There are thirty-nine books in the Old Testament, as they are divided in our English translations, and twenty-seven books in the New Testament. This is according to the Protestant division of Scripture.

THE OLD TESTAMENT WAS WRITTEN OVER A THOUSAND YEAR PERIOD

The Old Testament was composed from about 1,400 to 400 B.C. Thus, it took about one thousand years to complete the various books of the Old Testament. The first book written was Genesis or Job while the last book was likely Nehemiah.

BEFORE JESUS THERE WAS ONLY THE HEBREW SCRIPTURES!

Before the coming of Jesus Christ to the world there was no such thing as an "Old" Testament—there were only the Hebrew Scriptures. They were the only authoritative collection of sacred writings that existed. The Hebrew Scripture was the "Bible" of Jesus, as well as those living in His day.

This is made clear from the following words of Jesus to the religious leaders. He said.

> You search the Scriptures because you think that in them you have eternal life; and it is they that bear witness about me (John 5:39 ESV).

Note Jesus told them they search *the Scriptures*! He did not define what He meant by the term—He did not have to explain it. They knew exactly what He was talking about.

Furthermore, though these religious leaders disagreed with Jesus about many different issues, they were in agreement with Him as to the extent of the Scripture. That issue had been long-settled.

A NEW CHAPTER IN GOD'S REVELATION: A NEW TESTAMENT

Therefore, the extent of the Hebrew Scriptures was known by those living in Jesus' day. However, with His appearance into the world, a new chapter in the history of God's personal involvement with humanity was to be written—the "New" Testament.

THE LATEST REVELATION DOES NOT CONTRADICT THE EARLIER

The New Testament is new in the sense that it is the *latest* revelation from God. In other words, it is not new in the sense that it is different or contradictory to the Old Testament. Indeed, it merely continues God's revelation of Himself and His truth to the human race.

GOD'S FINAL REVELATION OF HIMSELF: JESUS CHRIST

We also note that the latest revelation, the New Testament, is God's *final* revelation to the human race. The Bible says.

> Long ago, at many times and in many ways, God spoke to our fathers by the prophets, but in these last days he has spoken to us by his Son, whom he appointed the heir of all things, through whom also he created the world (Hebrews 1:1,2 ESV).

The Old Testament prophets looked forward to the day when the Messiah, the Deliverer, would come to earth. This was their hope.

The New Testament records the fulfillment of that hope. It is the account of God becoming a human being in the Person of Jesus Christ. John wrote.

> No one has ever seen God, but the one and only Son, who is himself God and is in closest relationship with the Father, has made him known (John 1:18 NIV).

Do you want to know what God is like? Then look at Jesus. He explains God to us.

THE NEW TESTAMENT WAS WRITTEN DURING A SHORT PERIOD OF TIME

Let's look at the composition of the New Testament. To begin with, we find that the New Testament was written during a much shorter period of time than the Old Testament. The various books were composed from approximately A.D. 40 to A.D. 80.

The earliest New Testament book written is most likely one of four (Matthew, Galatians, 1 Thessalonians, or James). We are not certain which was composed first.

The last book written was probably the Book of Revelation. However, it is also possible that one of the other writings of John—Third

John—was written after the Book of Revelation. There is not enough evidence to be certain.

To sum up: It took about 1,000 years to compose the Old Testament, but only about 40 years for the entire New Testament.

SOME NEW TESTAMENT BOOKS WERE NOT ORIGINALLY WRITTEN FOR PUBLICATION

Some of the sacred writings that make up the New Testament were not originally written with the idea of publication, or public distribution. For example, Philemon is a short private letter to an individual. The writings of 2 and 3 John are also too short to properly be called books.

NEVERTHELESS THEY ARE GOD'S WORD

Even though the original intent for a few of these works may not have been publication, each of them carried God's divine authority. These divinely authoritative writings have now been collected and published into one book—the Bible.

OBSERVATION 2: THE BIBLE IS A DIVINE AND HUMAN BOOK

Next we will discover that the two main sections of the Bible, the Old and New Testament become one Book that is both divine and human.

From a human standpoint, over forty different authors wrote the books of the Bible. While made up of sixty-six separate books, the Bible is, in actuality, one book with *one* ultimate author behind it—*God* the Holy Spirit. This is the claim the Bible makes about itself.

SCRIPTURE CLAIMS TO BE GOD'S WORD!

This brings us to the next point. Scripture testifies to its own divine inspiration. Paul wrote.

> All Scripture is God-breathed and is useful for teaching, rebuking, correcting and training in righteousness, so that

the servant of God may be thoroughly equipped for every good work (2 Timothy 3:16-17 NIV).

Notice that *all* Scripture is breathed out by God and all of it is profitable. This is the claim of Scripture itself.

Peter wrote something similar. He put it this way.

> Above all, you must understand that no prophecy of Scripture came about by the prophet's own interpretation of things. For prophecy never had its origin in the human will, but prophets, though human, spoke from God as they were carried along by the Holy Spirit (2 Peter 1:20-21 NIV).

Note that the ultimate source was *not* the prophets own imagination or any human impulse. No, they were carried along by the Holy Spirit. He was behind all of their writings!

The Bible therefore is the Word of God written in the words of humans. This is the claim the Bible makes for itself.

THE BIBLE WAS WRITTEN IN THE THIRD PERSON

We find that this is borne out in the composition of Scripture. Although the Bible claims to be God's Word, it is written in the third person rather than the first person. For example, the first verse of Scripture reads.

> In the beginning God created the heavens and the earth (Genesis 1:1 KJV).

We do not find the personal pronoun "I" used.

Indeed, God did not say, "In the beginning *I* created." Instead God used human writers to compose His Word.

Again we emphasize that the Scriptures are a divine/human product. It is absolutely essential that this truth be understood.

THERE IS UNITY AND DIVERSITY IN THE BIBLE

Consequently, the Scripture shows both unity and diversity. It is a unity because one author, God, is behind the books. It is diverse because many human authors were used to compose the various books. Each had their own unique vocabulary and personality. This is reflected in their writings.

THE BIBLE WAS WRITTEN BY HUMAN BEINGS

What does this mean? Well, it means that God decided to use humans to record His truths to humanity. He did not use angels; God did not personally write the books of the Bible; the Scripture was not found on some hidden golden plates neither did it drop down from heaven. Instead, God used ordinary people guided by the Holy Spirit to produce His Word.

HOW CAN IT BE ERROR-FREE?

But doesn't this mean the Bible must contain errors since it was written by humans? Here's how the argument goes

Humans make mistakes;
The Bible was written by humans,
Therefore, Bible contains errors.

Right? No, wrong! Scripture says God supernaturally watched over the writings to produce a trustworthy account.

While humans can and do make mistakes, they *do not* have to make mistakes. In other words, humans can perform acts that are error free— such as me correctly spelling my own name.

Therefore, the Bible is the Word of God in the words of humans. The end result is an error free/trustworthy Book from the living God.

THIS IS NOT TOO HARD FOR GOD

Just a reminder—this is not too hard for God. The Lord has said.

> I am the Lord, the God of all mankind. Is anything too hard
> for me? (Jeremiah 32:27 NIV).

What do you think the answer is? Correct. The answer is, "No!"

OBSERVATION 3: THE BIBLE WAS NOT WRITTEN IN ANY SYSTEMATIC FORM

The two main sections of the Bible, the Old and New Testament, have become one Book. This Book is both divine and human—it records God's revelation of Himself to humanity.

This revelation is not written in the form of a systematic theology. In other words, there is not a section on God, on who we humans are, on sin, on angels, etc.

THE TRUTHS WERE PROGRESSIVELY REVEALED

Instead, the Bible consists of a number of historical and personal writings that reveal God's Person and plan to humanity. These truths were not all revealed at once. We will cite again a verse that we quoted earlier.

> In the past God spoke to our ancestors through the prophets
> at many times and in various ways, but in these last days
> he has spoken to us by his Son, whom he appointed heir
> of all things, and through whom also he made the universe
> (Hebrews 1:1,2 NIV).

Note that in many ways, and at many times, God revealed Himself to humanity. In other words, He revealed His truth progressively.

The end result is a story—a love story between God and the human race. In particular, it centers upon those humans who love and obey Him.

THE GREAT DRAMA IS ALL ABOUT GOD AND HIS PEOPLE

Have you ever been in a play? I have. I remember my Jr. High teacher, Mr. Smart, telling us actors, "You don't ever upstage the main characters!" The focus of any drama is *always* on the main participants.

God and humanity are the main players in this great drama recorded in the Bible. In particular, it is God and those humans who obey him. While the spotlight is on God and His people, there are others which enter the drama—such as angels. However, they are only mentioned insofar as they have something to do with the relationship of God and humanity. Therefore, our knowledge about this subject is limited because there is no attempt to answer our curiosity about them.

The same holds true for other nations and individuals mentioned in the Bible. They come and go off the stage but the focus is never on them. Indeed, it is always on God and those humans who are His chosen people.

Therefore, we learn certain things about the leaders, customs, political structure, wars, etc. of certain peoples but this is only in reference to the two main characters in the drama.

Why this emphasis? Again, it is because God has a special interest in those who serve Him!

IN THE OLD TESTAMENT ABRAHAM AND HIS DESCENDANTS ARE THE MAIN TOPIC

We can illustrate this as follows. In the Old Testament it was Abraham and his descendants, the nation of Israel, which is highlighted. The Old Testament chronicles their history and the dealings they had with the Lord.

GENESIS 1-11: MONUMENTAL EVENTS

For example, let's take a look at the Book of Genesis. In Genesis 1-11 we have monumental events listed; the creation of the heaven and the earth; the creation of the first humans; the explanation of how the perfect world became imperfect; the Genesis Flood; the Tower of Babel, etc.

GENESIS 12-50: FAMILY MATTERS: ABRAHAM AND HIS DESCENDANTS

While Genesis chapters 1-11 cover these monumental events with respect to the earth, its beginning, Fall, Flood, etc., the greater part of the Book of Genesis concentrates on one family—that of Abraham.

Indeed, chapters 12-50 describe what we can call "family matters." Therefore, the emphasis in the Book of Genesis is on this one family and their relationship with God.

NEW TESTAMENT: JESUS THE MESSIAH

We find a similar emphasis in the New Testament. It is concerned with God becoming a human being in the Person of Jesus Christ. The New Testament also highlights the activities of those who believe in Him. Again we find that the emphasis is upon God's relationship with His people.

Consequently, in Scripture, "bit players" come and go, on and off the stage. The focus, the bright lights, is always on God and His special people—Abraham's descendants in the Old Testament, and Jesus, and those who believe in Him, the New Testament.

This brings us to our next observation . . .

OBSERVATION 4: THE BIBLE IS TRUE, BUT NOT EXHAUSTIVE

The Bible, in two testaments, was written by human instruments, who were divinely inspired by God. Scripture was written as an unfolding story which reveals truth about God to us.

The Bible claims to reveal truth about God and His creation. In addition, it contains *everything* that God *wants* us to know about whom He is, and who we are.

THE WRITERS WERE SELECTIVE IN WHAT THEY WROTE

However, Scripture does not tell us everything we would *like* to know about Him—only the things that we *need* to know.

For example, the Apostle John told his readers that he did not record *all* the acts of Jesus that he witnessed but rather was selective in what he recorded. He wrote.

> Jesus performed many other signs in the presence of his disciples, which are not recorded in this book. But these are written that you may believe that Jesus is the Messiah, the Son of God, and that by believing you may have life in his name (John 20:30,31 NIV).

We also read the following at the end of John's gospel.

> Jesus did many other things as well. If every one of them were written down, I suppose that even the whole world would not have room for the books that would be written (John 21:25 NIV).

Therefore, everything we *need* to know about God, or ourselves, is found in Scripture. It contains *sufficient* truth about who God is, who we are, and how we can enter into a right relationship with Him.

What we *need* to know—not what we want to know. This is what is contained in Scripture.

TRUTH IS TRUTH WHETHER RELIGIOUS OR HISTORICAL

Something else must be noted. While some people want to make a distinction between "religious" truth and other kinds of truth, there is only one kind of truth. Spiritual, or religious truth, is just as factual as any other area of truth.

Thus, the Bible is accurate in all that it says—whether it is of a historical nature, such as Pontius Pilate being the Governor of Judea, or of a spiritual nature—Jesus died for the sins of the world, etc.

CONTEXT, CONTEXT, CONTEXT

The Bible consists of direct statements made by God as well as statements from humans who spoke for Him. For example, the prophets spoke with God's divine authority. Thus, when we say the Bible is God's Word, it does not mean that God personally spoke *every* word that is contained in the Bible.

THE BIBLE RECORDS LIES

However, there is something else we must emphasize—the Bible also accurately records lies and untrue statements made by individuals. In addition, it also records sinful deeds that were committed. While the Bible does not endorse these false statements and sinful deeds, it accurately records what was said and what took place.

For example, Jesus said the following to the religious leaders of His day.

> You are of your father the Devil, and you want to carry out your father's desires. He was a murderer from the beginning and has not stood in the truth, because there is no truth in him. When he tells a lie, he speaks from his own nature, because he is a liar and the father of liars (John 8:44 HCSB).

According to Jesus, the devil is always a liar. Therefore, any statement in Scripture that accurately records his words will always contain lies!

Thus, not every statement in Scripture is true and not every act recorded was done with God's blessing. Lies and sinful acts are recorded because they played a part in telling God's unfolding story of humanity. They are recorded accurately—but this does not mean God endorses the statement or action. This must be understood.

In sum, the Scriptures are selective in the truth that it records—what is taught is trustworthy in that what is recorded truly happened or was truly said. Yet, we must be careful to read each and every statement in its context.

OBSERVATION 5: THE BIBLE WAS WRITTEN FOR EVERYONE TO UNDERSTAND

The Bible in two testaments, written by human beings who were divinely inspired by God, written as an unfolding story, reveals selective truth about God to us—it is everything we need to know about ourselves.

WE CAN UNDERSTAND IT!

The good news is that Scripture has been written in a way that it can be read and understood by everyone—not just a select few. The message of the Bible is for all people, in all countries, and for all time.

Jesus told His original disciples to go out into the entire world and teach and preach His message. The Gospel according to Matthew ends with Jesus making this command.

> Then Jesus came near and said to them, "All authority has been given to Me in heaven and on earth. Go, therefore, and make disciples of all nations, baptizing them in the name of the Father and of the Son and of the Holy Spirit, teaching them to observe everything I have commanded you. And remember, I am with you always, to the end of the age" (Matthew 28:18-20 HCSB).

Therefore, all of those who believe in Jesus are instructed to become His disciples. They are to learn about Him as well as teach others the truth. This, of course, assumes that we can understand His truth.

JESUS COMMANDED BELIEVERS TO LEARN FROM HIM

Jesus gave the following invitation to believers.

> Come to Me, all of you who are weary and burdened, and I will give you rest. All of you, take up My yoke and learn from Me, because I am gentle and humble in heart, and you will find rest for yourselves. For My yoke is easy and My burden is light (Matthew 11:28-30 HCSB).

We *can* learn from Him—all of us. Again we find the Bible assuming that we are able to do this.

JESUS SAID THE PEOPLE SHOULD HAVE KNOWN ABOUT HIS DEATH

On the day of His resurrection we read the following words of Jesus to two disciples walking with Him on the road to Emmaus.

> He said to them, "How unwise and slow you are to believe in your hearts all that the prophets have spoken! Didn't the Messiah have to suffer these things and enter into His glory?" Then beginning with Moses and all the Prophets, He interpreted for them the things concerning Himself in all the Scriptures (Luke 24:25-27 HCSB).

They should have known what was going to happen to the Messiah but they did not. This, statement, however, assumes they could have known!

THE PEOPLE REFUSED TO UNDERSTAND THE TRUTH ABOUT JESUS

On another occasion we read Jesus saying.

> As He approached and saw the city, He wept over it, saying, "If you knew this day what would bring peace—but now it is hidden from your eyes. For the days will come on you when your enemies will build an embankment

against you, surround you, and hem you in on every side. They will crush you and your children within you to the ground, and they will not leave one stone on another in you, because you did not recognize the time of your visitation." (Luke 19:41-42 HCSB).

The people could have understood but they chose not to. Therefore, we again find that we can understand the truths of Scripture.

THEY REFUSED TO LET JESUS PROTECT THEM

Finally, Jesus stressed the following to the inhabitants of Jerusalem.

Jerusalem, Jerusalem, you who kill the prophets and stone those sent to you, how often I have longed to gather your children together, as a hen gathers her chicks under her wings, and you were not willing (Matthew 23:37 NIV).

They would not let Him protect them. Could they have? Yes. But they were not willing.

Is the message understandable? Yes. Indeed, we are all held responsible for what the Scripture says.

In sum, these five observations should be our starting point as we seek to understand what the Bible is all about.

SUMMARY TO QUESTION 1
WHAT IS THE BIBLE?

The Bible is one large book made up of sixty-six smaller books. It is the divine library—the Word of God to humanity. The Word of God has come to humanity in two testaments—the Old and the New.

Five basic observations need to be made about this Book.

To begin with, God did not reveal all of these truths at once. Instead, He revealed them in these particular books, through a number of human writers, over a fifteen-hundred-year span.

The result is the Bible: The Word of God written in the words of human beings. Therefore, it is a Book that is both human and divine.

As we look at the Bible, we find that it was not written in any systematic form of doctrine or teaching, but rather consists of God's revelation of Himself throughout history.

Although the Bible does not contain everything we would like to know about God, it does contain everything that is necessary.

Finally, Scripture was written for everyone to read and understand—it is not just for the elite.

QUESTION 2

Is it Important to Consider the Claims of the Bible? (15 Reasons Why)

In the Book of Ecclesiastes, written about 950 B.C., the writer made a comment on the number of books which have been composed. He put it this way.

> Of making many books there is no end (Ecclesiastes 12:12 NIV).

He complained about the number of books that had been written.

As we move through history, we find this idea repeated.

Indeed, there was a first century Roman writer who complained that it would take him an entire lifetime—not to go through all the books that were available—but rather just to get through all the *catalogs* of books!

Indeed, there is *no* end to the making of books.

SO WHY THIS ONE BOOK?

With so many books written in the history of humanity why should we pay attention to this one Book, the Bible?

Here's why. The Bible is not humanity's thoughts about God—it is God revealing His truth to humanity. Because it claims to be the *sole* revelation of God to the human race, and because the consequences for rejecting the message are so great, it is crucial that people consider the claims that the Bible makes.

THE NEED FOR THE BIBLE ILLUSTRATED

Human beings have come to conclusions on so many topics but not on the subject of whether or not God exists! In fact, they cannot and do not, come to any conclusion on divine truth. We can illustrate by simply examining the following belief systems.

AGNOSTICS DON'T KNOW IF GOD OR GODS EXIST

Agnostics do not know whether or not God exists. They are "without knowledge" when it comes to knowing if a God or gods exist. Agnostics just don't know. Many people fall into this category.

ATHEISTS CLAIM THEY DO KNOW: GOD DOES NOT EXIST

Contrary to agnostics, atheists claim to know whether or not God exists—they insist He does *not*. Sophisticated atheists understand they really cannot make this claim as a statement of fact. Why? It is the fallacy of categorical denial. No human being has the knowledge to make such a comprehensive statement.

Indeed, for one to be in a position to make such a statement *they* would have to have all knowledge—and this would make *them* God!

Rather the atheist will claim there is not sufficient evidence to believe that a God or gods exists.

THEISTS ALSO CLAIM TO KNOW: GOD DOES EXIST

Contrary to the agnostics, theists do know whether or not a God or gods exist. And contrary to the atheists, theists believe that God or gods do exist.

With these different beliefs that humans hold we need something to tell us whether or not God exists. We have it—the Bible. It is God's revelation to us. In other words, it is not our ideas about whether or not He exists.

THERE ARE MANY REASONS WHY WE SHOULD CONSIDER THE CLAIMS OF THE BIBLE

There are a number of reasons as to why it is important to consider the claims of Holy Scripture. We will note fifteen of them. They include the following.

REASON 1: THE BIBLE CLAIMS TO BE GOD'S WORD TO HUMANITY: IT IS HIS BOOK

The Bible is often called the "Good Book." However, it is more than a "good book" for it claims to be "God's Book." The Bible claims to be the very Word of God, that is, His supernatural communication to the human race. Indeed, over five thousand times in the Old Testament alone we find such phrases as, "Thus says the Lord," or "God said."

For example, the beginning verses from the Book of Jeremiah make it clear that it is more than a mere human work. It reads.

> The words of Jeremiah son of Hilkiah, one of the priests at
> Anathoth in the territory of Benjamin. The word of the Lord
> came to him in the thirteenth year of the reign of Josiah son
> of Amon king of Judah (Jeremiah 1:1,2 NIV).

Notice these first two verses inform us that God "began" to speak to Jeremiah. The remainder of the Book of Jeremiah claims to record God "continuing" to speak to the prophet.

Other biblical books make similar claims—God has spoken, and His Words are recorded in a particular book. Isaiah the prophet wrote.

> I am Isaiah, the son of Amoz. And this is the message that I was given about Judah and Jerusalem when Uzziah, Jotham, Ahaz, and Hezekiah were the kings of Judah: The LORD has said, "Listen, heaven and earth! The children I raised have turned against me" (Isaiah 1:1-2 CEV).

Isaiah claimed that God spoke to him and that he recorded God's message.

Hosea made a similar claim.

> I am Hosea son of Beeri. When Uzziah, Jotham, Ahaz, and Hezekiah were the kings of Judah, and when Jeroboam son of Jehoash was king of Israel, the LORD spoke this message to me (Hosea 1:1 CEV).

Notice what he said, "The Lord spoke this message to me." God spoke— humans recorded His words and deeds.

IT IS GOD'S *ONLY* REVELATION OF HIMSELF

There is more. Scripture claims to be God's unique revelation to humanity. Indeed, the Bible is the *only* sacred book where the One True God has revealed Himself. This one Book alone is God's written Word to the human race. There are no other written sources of divine truth apart from the Bible. None.

All other so-called sacred books are mere pretenders. No other religious book gives us God's divine truth—this includes the Qur'an, the Book of Mormon, the Hindu Scriptures, or so-called later revelation to Christians. No other book, no human being, can add or subtract to what God has revealed.

Therefore, out of all of the countless millions of books that have ever been written, the Bible is the only one which has God's authority behind it. This is not our claim—it is the Bible's. We don't say it—the Bible does!

THE WARNING FROM THE BIBLE NOT TO ADD OR SUBTRACT

Indeed, Scripture gives a warning not to add to it or subtract from it. In the Book of Deuteronomy God commanded.

> You must not add anything to what I command you or take anything away from it, so that you may keep the commands of the Lord your God I am giving you (Deuteronomy 4:2 HCSB).

The people were warned not to tamper with God's Word.

The New Testament says something similar. We read the following stern warning in the Book of Revelation.

> I testify to everyone who hears the prophetic words of this book: If anyone adds to them, God will add to him the plagues that are written in this book. And if anyone takes away from the words of this prophetic book, God will take away his share of the tree of life and the holy city, written in this book (Revelation 22:18,19 NIV).

Strong words, but they are His words! These are God's claims—not ours. We are merely His ambassadors, His messengers, as the Apostle Paul noted when he wrote.

> Therefore, we are ambassadors for Christ, certain that God is appealing through us. We plead on Christ's behalf, "Be reconciled to God" (2 Corinthians 5:20 HCSB).

We are faithfully passing along His claims. We did not invent them.

REASON 2: ALL CHRISTIAN DOCTRINE, OR TEACHING, IS BASED SOLELY UPON THE SCRIPTURE

Not only is the Bible the one Book that God has given to humanity, each and every doctrine that Christians believe is based *solely* upon the teaching of Scripture. Indeed, it is the *only* source to where we can go to find authoritative answers to our spiritual questions.

Thus, appeal must be made to the Bible alone to determine our belief system. In other words, without the Bible there is no Christian belief system. Christian teaching, or Christian doctrine, therefore, stands or falls on the authority of the Bible. Consequently, what the Bible says is of the utmost importance.

In sum, it is only from Scripture that we discover the unique teachings of the Christian faith. There is no other source. Indeed, neither popes, nor church councils, nor church tradition, can give us authoritative Christian doctrine.

WE ARE TO KNOW WHAT WE BELIEVE

We also find that the Bible commands us to know what we believe about God, as well as why we believe it. We read.

> But in your hearts revere Christ as Lord. Always be prepared to give an answer to everyone who asks you to give the reason for the hope that you have. But do this with gentleness and respect (1 Peter 3:15 NIV).

How are we going to know what we believe? We can only know this by studying the Bible—our only source for Christian belief.

WE ARE TO WEIGH AND EVALUATE THINGS

The Bible also commands us to "test" the things which are taught to us. Paul wrote to the Corinthians about this necessity.

> Test yourselves and find out if you really are true to your faith (2 Corinthians 13:5 CEV).

How do we test things? It is through carefully examining the Bible.

In another letter, he stated it this way.

> Put everything to the test. Accept what is good (1 Thessalonians 5:21 CEV).

Everything should be tested—everything!

The Apostle John wrote something similar.

> Dear friends, don't believe everyone who claims to have the Spirit of God. Test them all to find out if they really do come from God. Many false prophets have already gone out into the world (1 John 4:1 CEV).

Again, what is the standard that we test all things by? It is the Word of God alone.

REASON 3: THE BIBLE GIVES THE FINAL ANSWERS TO LIFE'S MOST IMPORTANT QUESTIONS

Because the Bible is the sole revelation from God to the human race, it is not only where all Christian teaching comes from, it also gives us the *final* answers to our deepest questions.

Indeed, for centuries people have turned to the Bible for the ultimate answers to the basic questions of life: Where did we human beings come from? Why are we here on Planet Earth? What will happen to us when we die?

The Bible answers these questions.

THE WORLD WAS CREATED PERFECT

The Bible alone explains our present world. Scripture tells us that a personal infinite God originally created a perfect world. After describing the six days of creation we read.

And God saw everything that he had made and that it was very good (Genesis 1:31 God's Word).

Everything was created perfect in the beginning. There is a double superlative here—it was "very good."

GENESIS 3: THE FALL OF HUMANITY

However, the world became imperfect by the sin of Adam and Eve (recorded in Genesis 3). This explains that the world we now live in is abnormal. In other words, it is *not* the perfect world God created.

THERE IS A NEW WORLD COMING

The Scripture gives us good news—a new world is coming! This will be a perfect world which will be free from evil, suffering, and death! The Book of Romans explains it this way.

> For all creation is waiting eagerly for that future day when God will reveal who his children really are. Against its will, all creation was subjected to God's curse. But with eager hope, the creation looks forward to the day when it will join God's children in glorious freedom from death and decay. For we know that all creation has been groaning as in the pains of childbirth right up to the present time. And we believers also groan, even though we have the Holy Spirit within us as a foretaste of future glory, for we long for our bodies to be released from sin and suffering. We, too, wait with eager hope for the day when God will give us our full rights as his adopted children, including the new bodies he has promised us (Romans 8:19-23 NLT).

Notice what this passage tells us. All of God's creation is waiting for that future time when the curse of sin will be removed. That day is coming! Until it occurs, the human race, as well as all creation, is longing for that that time.

The Book of Revelation also makes this prediction about the wonderful days ahead for those who believe.

> I heard a loud voice shout from the throne: God's home is now with his people. He will live with them, and they will be his own. Yes, God will make his home among his people. He will wipe all tears from their eyes, and there will be no more death, suffering, crying, or pain. These things of the past are gone forever. Then the one sitting on the throne said: I am making everything new. Write down what I have said. My words are true and can be trusted (Revelation 21:3-5 CEV).

This is the future for those of us who believe—no more sorrow, crying, or pain. Yet, we only know about these fabulous truths from the Bible.

Therefore, the Bible is important in that it gives us the final answer on all topics which it deals with!

WHY THIS IS NECESSARY

As human beings, all of us have a limited perspective. In fact, none of us are in a position to give final, definitive answers about anything. Any ultimate answer must come from outside of this world! The good news is that we have these answers—from the living God Himself.

Therefore, a third reason as to why the Bible is important—it alone gives us final answers to our deepest questions!

REASON 4: ONLY THE SCRIPTURE TELLS US WHAT GOD IS LIKE

Here's one of the questions in which we need a final answer—Who is God? What is He like?

Only the Bible tells us what the living God is like. This is not something that we can discover on our own. In fact, without God's divine revelation, we would know next to nothing about Him.

This is illustrated in the Book of Job. We find that Job and his three friends attempted to understand why he was suffering. Their attempts were without the benefit of God's viewpoint on the matter. When God finally responded to their words, we discover Him saying the following about their efforts.

> Then the Lord spoke to Job out of the storm. He said: "Who is this that obscures my plans with words without knowledge? Brace yourself like a man; I will question you, and you shall answer me. "Where were you when I laid the earth's foundation? Tell me, if you understand" (Job 38:1-4 NIV).

The Lord called their conclusions "words without knowledge." They were trying to understand Job's problem without the benefit of God's viewpoint. Their conclusions were worthless—as are all others who do not have God's perspective.

Basically God asked them, "Where were you when I created everything?" If they were not there, and have no knowledge about how He created the material universe, then how can they tell God how He should operate the moral side of the universe? Simply put, they cannot.

This is another indication of our need for an authoritative Scripture. We cannot understand what God has done, or what He is like, unless He reveals it to us. It is only in the Bible that we can find infallible answers to these questions.

THERE IS ONLY ONE GOD WHO EXISTS

There is another thing that we learn. According to the Bible there is only "one" God which exists. Isaiah the prophet recorded God saying.

> My people, you are my witnesses and my chosen servant. I want you to know me, to trust me, and understand that I alone am God. I have always been God; there can be no others (Isaiah 43:10 CEV).

Notice He says, "There can be no others."

In another place, the prophet recorded the Lord saying.

> I am the LORD All-Powerful, the first and the last, the one and only God (Isaiah 44:6 CEV).

There are no other gods who exist. None. This is the claim of Scripture.

GOD IS SPIRIT

The one God who exists is spirit. Jesus said.

> For God is Spirit, so those who worship him must worship in spirit and in truth (John 4:24 NLT).

A spirit does not have any physical form. Jesus made this clear to His disciples when He appeared to them in a resurrected body.

> While Jesus' disciples were talking about what had happened, Jesus appeared and greeted them. They were frightened and terrified because they thought they were seeing a ghost. But Jesus said, "Why are you so frightened? Why do you doubt? Look at my hands and my feet and see who I am! Touch me and find out for yourselves. Ghosts don't have flesh and bones as you see I have" (Luke 24:36-39 CEV).

A "spirit" or a "ghost" does not have any physical form as Jesus had in His resurrected body. God, by nature, is an invisible eternal spirit. We only know this from the testimony of Scripture.

WE ARE NOT TO MAKE IMAGES OF HIM

Because God does not have any physical form, we are *not* to make idols or images of Him. We read the following in the Ten Commandments.

> You must not make for yourself an idol of any kind or an image of anything in the heavens or on the earth or in the

sea. You must not bow down to them or worship them, for I, the Lord your God, am a jealous God who will not tolerate your affection for any other gods (Exodus 20:4-5 NLT).

God is very clear on this subject—we are not to make images of Him!

HUMANS HAVE MADE GOD IN OUR IMAGE

Unfortunately, we human beings often make God in our image. In other words, we mold and shape Him in the way we think He should be.

For example, people often say, "I think God is like . . ." and then they fill in the blank. When humans do this, they are assuming they can know what God is like. However, as we have seen, humans come to no consensus or agreement on the matter. None.

Back to what the Lord said to Job and his friends. When people do this sort of thing they are uttering "words without knowledge." Indeed, God alone must tell us what He is like. Our opinions are worthless.

REASON 5: THE BIBLE TELLS US WHAT GOD EXPECTS FROM US: BELIEVE IN HIM THROUGH JESUS CHRIST

Scripture also informs us what God expects from humanity. The message of the Scripture is clear in this respect. There is only one God who exists, and there is only one way to have a personal relationship with Him. It is only through Jesus Christ that an individual can experience the one, true God. Jesus said.

> I am the way, the truth, and the life. No one comes to the Father except through Me (John 14:6 NKJV).

The Bible was written for the purpose of creating belief in God through the Person of Jesus Christ. The Apostle John explained the purpose of his gospel in the following statement.

Jesus performed many other signs in the presence of his disciples, which are not recorded in this book. But these are written that you may believe that Jesus is the Messiah, the Son of God, and that by believing you may have life in his name (John 20:30,31 NIV).

John wrote his gospel so that people would believe in Jesus. He made his purpose clear.

The Bible says that salvation is in Christ alone. The Apostle Peter said the following to a group of religious leaders who challenged his preaching about Christ.

And there is salvation in no one else, for there is no other name under heaven given among men by which we must be saved (Acts 4:12 ESV).

The Apostle John emphasized that a person must believe in God the Son, Jesus Christ, to have a relationship with God the Father. He wrote.

No one who denies the Son has the Father; whoever acknowledges the Son has the Father also (1 John 2:23 NIV).

The consistent message of the New Testament is that it is only through the Person of Jesus Christ that an individual can experience the one, true God. All other ways are false.

Paul wrote the following to the church at Rome about the necessity of believing in Jesus. He said.

For "Anyone who calls on the name of the Lord will be saved." But how can they call on him to save them unless they believe in him? And how can they believe in him if they have never heard about him? And how can they hear about him unless someone tells them? And how will anyone go and tell them without being sent? That is what the

> Scriptures mean when they say, "How beautiful are the feet of those who bring good news!" But not everyone welcomes the Good News, for Isaiah the prophet said, "Lord, who has believed our message?" Yet faith comes from listening to this message of good news—the Good News about Christ (Romans 10:13-17 NLT).

There are a number of important points that we can discover from this passage.

First, one must call upon the name of Christ, or believe in Him, to be saved. A person must believe He is whom He claimed to be.

To do this, one must first hear about Him. Someone must tell them. They must hear a preacher or read some message about Jesus. Without hearing about Jesus, they cannot believe.

Paul also wrote.

> For there is one God and one intermediary between God and humanity, Christ Jesus, himself human (1 Timothy 2:5 NET).

There is only one God, and only one way to reach the one God—through Jesus Christ. This is the clear message of the New Testament.

ILLUSTRATION: NOBODY CAN SWIM FROM CALIFORNIA TO HAWAII

Here's a way to illustrate this truth. It is about 2,500 miles from the west coast of the United States to Honolulu, Hawaii. Let's say you and two friends decide to swim from the coast of California to Hawaii.

The first swimmer swims about 250 feet and then stops and starts treading water. The next swimmer swims about 500 feet, twice as far as the first swimmer. However, after 500 feet the second swimmer also stops and starts treading water. Finally, you begin your swim and you get about 5,000 feet from the shore before you start treading water.

You look back with pride that you have gone twenty times farther than the first swimmer, and ten times as far as the second. You may have done better than each of them—but you are still 2,500 miles short of the mark! The three of you are going to drown!

This illustrates a biblical truth. No matter how good we may be, we are not good enough to please God! The Bible makes this clear. It says.

> For all have sinned and fall short of the glory of God (Romans 3:23).

All of us have fallen short. None of us is perfect. How does sin pay off? Death! The Bible says.

> For the payoff of sin is death, but the gift of God is eternal life in Christ Jesus our Lord (Romans 6:23).

While sin pays off in death, God gives the gift of eternal life to those who believe in Jesus. We do not have to try to swim to Hawaii—to make it on our own. He Himself takes us where we need to go!

REASON 6: SCRIPTURE PROVIDES A BASIS FOR A SCIENTIFIC UNDERSTANDING OF THE UNIVERSE

Though this may surprise some, the Bible has served as a basis for modern scientific pursuits. In fact, modern science was born in the seventeenth century because of a belief in an unchanging God of order, purpose and consistency—the God that is portrayed in the Bible.

It was from this basis that scientists could study the form and function of the universe as it now exists. Therefore, modern science has the Bible to thank for its origins.

The Bible itself emphasizes that the universe is a testimony to God's existence and power. The psalmist wrote about this when he said the following.

> The heavens declare the glory of God; the skies proclaim the work of his hands. Day after day they pour forth speech; night after night they reveal knowledge. They have no speech, they use no words; no sound is heard from them. Yet their voice goes out into all the earth, their words to the ends of the world (Psalm 19:1-4 NIV).

The visible creation is a constant testimony to the power and majesty of God. Consequently, humans are without excuse. The Apostle Paul makes this clear.

> For since the creation of the world God's invisible qualities—his eternal power and divine nature—have been clearly seen, being understood from what has been made, so that people are without excuse (Romans 1:20 NIV).

The testimony to the creative power of God is everywhere. Humans, therefore, know that there is a God who exists.

WHAT DO WE REALLY KNOW ABOUT ANYTHING?

But who is this God? Science certainly cannot give us the answers to this ultimate question about God's identity. Or for that matter, there are so many things to which science can give us no real answer.

This is illustrated in a statement made by Dr. Edward Teller, the father of the hydrogen bomb. He described the progress of science from the Second World War until the year 1970 in the following way.

> Practically everything that for years we believed to be true has been proven false or incorrect by subsequent discovery. In fact there is only one statement that I would now dare to make positively: There is absolutely nothing faster than the speed of light—maybe.[1]

---

1. *Readers Digest*, September 1970, p. 20

This certainly does not give us much confidence in the assured results of science!

This statement echoes the verses we previously mentioned—the famous words God spoke to Job and his three friends.

> Then the LORD spoke to Job out of the storm. He said:
> "Who is this that obscures my plans with words without
> knowledge? Prepare to defend yourself; I will question you,
> and you shall answer me. "Where were you when I laid the
> earth's foundation? Tell me, if you understand" (Job 38:1-4).

Words without knowledge! The point is clear—we humans cannot know what happened at the beginning, who the Creator is, what He did, how we humans came about, etc., unless God tells us. No human being was there to observe it, and thus no human being knows what really happened.

Science, therefore, cannot provide any answers to these questions because the beginning of the universe was a "one-off" event. There is no chance of repeating or reproducing it.

However, the One who was there, God Himself, does provide us this information. Where? It is found in the Bible! This is where we discover these truths.

Jesus, God the Son, made a similar statement to the one we find in Job. In a private conversation which He had with the religious leader Nicodemus, Jesus said the following.

> If I have told you earthly things and you do not believe, how
> can you believe if I tell you heavenly things (John 3:12 ESV).

If we cannot understand things pertaining to the earth—how it was formed, how human life came about, etc.—then how are we going to understand eternal things? How are we going to know who God is, what He is like, etc.? The simple answer is that we cannot know any of these things on a purely human level. We simply do not have that capability.

However, we can know the answer to these and other monumental questions because God has given us the answers—in the Bible.

ARE WE HERE BY CHANCE OR DESIGN?

In fact, Scripture tells us over and over again that we are not a product of blind chance. Indeed, we have been made for a purpose. The Book of Revelation says.

> Our Lord and God, you are worthy to receive glory, honor, and power. You created all things, and by your decision they are and were created (Revelation 4:11 CEV).

The universe, and everything in it, was formed by the will of the Lord. We know this because the Bible tells us so. John wrote about Jesus' part in the creation of the universe.

> Through him all things were made; without him nothing was made that has been made (John 1:3 NIV).

God the Son was the Creator—the One who became a human being in the Person of Jesus Christ.

THE CONSEQUENCES IF WE ARE HERE BY BLIND CHANCE RATHER THAN DESIGN

Lest we think that this truth is not important, or somehow irrelevant to our daily lives, we should consider the results of accepting the idea that we are not here by God's direct design, but rather are a product of blind chance.

If the theory of atheistic evolution is correct, which means that everything is here as a result of blind chance, then it has far-reaching consequences for the Christian faith as well as for all of humanity.

The following are some of the logical results of accepting the modern atheistic theory of evolution.

CONSEQUENCE 1: THERE IS NO GOD

To begin with, the God of the Bible does not exist if everything in the universe is merely a result of a series of fortunate circumstances in the past history of the earth. Indeed, no God is necessary if everything exists because of blind chance.

CONSEQUENCE 2: THE BIBLE IS WRONG

The Bible repeatedly says we are here as a result of the direct creation by God. If we are not, then the Bible is wrong about this issue. If it is wrong on this, then it may be wrong on everything else which it teaches. Simply put, we could not trust it concerning *anything* that it says.

CONSEQUENCE 3: LIFE AROSE BY CHANCE

Life as we know it would be a result of blind chance rather than God's direct design—if the biblical account of creation is not true. We would then worship the "god of chance" rather than the God of the Bible since our existence would be attributed to chance alone.

Thus, life has no real meaning. Indeed, we are simply a product of lucky circumstances—if the Bible is wrong about God creating everything "in the beginning."

CONSEQUENCE 4: THERE IS NO NEED FOR A SAVIOR

Obviously, if life is a result of blind chance, or good luck, then there would be no need for a Savior since there would be no such thing as sin or evil. The death of Jesus Christ would be meaningless since there is no sin to be forgiven. Jesus' coming to the earth would have no significance whatsoever—if the Bible has this wrong.

CONSEQUENCE 5: THERE IS NO BASIS OF RIGHT OR WRONG

We humans would have no real basis of right and wrong—if the Bible is incorrect about God creating the universe. Indeed, if everything is a result of blind chance, then this leaves us without any moral standard. In other words, there is nobody to tell us good from evil, right from wrong. This is another of the consequences of accepting the idea that we are here by blind chance.

CONSEQUENCE 6: HUMANKIND HAS NO GENUINE HOPE FOR THE FUTURE

Finally, we would be without any genuine hope for the future if the biblical account of creation is incorrect. Indeed, we would have no purpose for living our lives or looking forward to what takes place after this life is over. In other words, we are living without hope! We are born, we live, and then we die. That's it. Life is ultimately meaningless.

The above would be some of the logical results if the Bible was wrong with respect as to how the world came into being. Consequently, our motto would be something like, "Eat, drink, and be merry, for tomorrow we may die."

Life would be reduced to something like this—if everything we see and experience is merely a result of blind unguided chance. Truly, this is a depressing thought.

THE GOOD NEWS

The good news, however, is that the Bible is right! We are not here by blind chance but rather by God's direct design. Life is not merely a meaningless exercise. Life has a meaning, a purpose.

Yet we only know about the meaning and purpose of life from the Bible. It is only from the pages of Scripture that we can find the answers. This is a further reason as to why it is so important to consider the claims of the Bible.

REASON 7: THE STORY OF THE BIBLE ENCOMPASSES ALL OF HUMAN HISTORY FROM GOD'S PERSPECTIVE

There is more. Scripture does not merely tell us how we got here, the beginning of human history, it also informs us about the end of human history on this earth.

The Bible speaks of the infinite personal God creating the heavens and the earth in the beginning (Genesis 1 and 2), and also records the creation of a new heaven and a new earth after the destruction of this present earth (Revelation 21, 22).

The Scripture informs us what will happen. We read the following in the Book of Revelation.

> Then I saw "a new heaven and a new earth," for the first heaven and the first earth had passed away, and there was no longer any sea. I saw the Holy City, the new Jerusalem, coming down out of heaven from God, prepared as a bride beautifully dressed for her husband (Revelation 21:1-2 NIV).

The entire history of the human race, past, present, and future, is thus chronicled for us in the pages of Scripture.

THE BIBLE TELLS US HOW GOD SEES HISTORY

While the Bible records the sweep of human history, it is important that we understand that the history recorded in the Bible is from God's perspective. In other words, we discover what is important to God when we study the pages of the Bible.

We find this truth illustrated in the first two verses in the third chapter of Luke's gospel. It reads as follows.

> In the fifteenth year of the reign of Tiberius Caesar—when Pontius Pilate was governor of Judea, Herod tetrarch of Galilee, his brother Philip tetrarch of Iturea and Traconitis,

and Lysanias tetrarch of Abilene—during the high-priest-hood of Annas and Caiaphas, the word of God came to John son of Zechariah in the wilderness (Luke 3:1-2 NIV).

Notice what we find here. There are seven historical figures mentioned including Caesar, Pontius Pilate the governor of Judea, Herod and various rulers, and the names of the high priests.

Yet we discover that the only purpose for them being mentioned was to inform us about the time when the word of the Lord came to a man named John who was living in the wilderness.

This is highly instructive. From God's viewpoint it is *not* the ruler of the known world, the governor of a province, or the various rulers or priests who are important. No, it is the man of God, John, through whom the Word of God came. He is one who is highlighted from God's perspective—not these other individuals who were so important at that time. God's viewpoint is certainly not the same as the viewpoint the secular world has.

THE LIFE OF KING SAUL IS SEEN FROM TWO PERSPECTIVES

Another example of this can be seen in the life of the first king of Israel, Saul. The Old Testament books of First and Second Samuel basically give us the secular view of history. In other words, they would relate history from the vantage point of someone living at the time.

However, the Book of Chronicles looks at the same events but it does so from God's perspective—the divine view.

When we look at the amount of space devoted to Saul, the first king of Israel, we can see the difference between God's perspective and the human perspective.

THE PEOPLE DEMANDED A KING

We are told that the people of Israel came to the prophet Samuel and demanded a king—they wanted to be just like all the other nations.

The Bible explains what took place when Samuel brought their request before the Lord.

> But when they said, "Give us a king to lead us," this displeased Samuel; so he prayed to the Lord. And the Lord told him: "Listen to all that the people are saying to you; it is not you they have rejected, but they have rejected me as their king. As they have done from the day I brought them up out of Egypt until this day, forsaking me and serving other gods, so they are doing to you" (1 Samuel 8:6-8 NIV).

Notice that the prophet Samuel, displeased with their request, brought it before the Lord. The Lord told him that the people had not rejected Samuel but actually had rejected Him by requesting a king. Therefore, we find that their choice, Saul, was *not* God's man for the job.

Saul is then introduced to us in the next chapter. His rule is recorded throughout the rest of the book of First Samuel. The last chapter records his death.

Therefore, in the secular view of history, there are some twenty-three chapters devoted to Saul—the choice of the people to be their king. He is one of the main subjects throughout this book.

GOD'S VIEW OF SAUL

Now let's contrast this with God's view of history as found in First Chronicles. Instead of twenty-three chapters, we find only one short chapter of fourteen verses dedicated to Saul! His epitaph at the end of the chapter reads as follows.

> Saul died because he was unfaithful to the Lord; he did not keep the word of the Lord and even consulted a medium for guidance, and did not inquire of the Lord. So the Lord put him to death and turned the kingdom over to David son of Jesse (1 Chronicles 10:13-14 NIV).

The contrast could not be greater! Saul is the main character throughout the Book of First Samuel—the secular view of events. Yet in God's view there is only one short chapter about the man.

Furthermore, the only reason he is even mentioned at all is to get to David—the man whom God had chosen. Otherwise we would have never heard about Saul.

This is a great lesson for all of us! God's view of things is not the same as the secular view. Let us never forget this.

REASON 8: THE BIBLE PROVIDES A PURPOSE FOR HISTORY

The Bible not only gives us God's view of history it also gives a purpose for history. From Scripture we find that history is not merely a series of random unrelated events. As the Bible records it, history has meaning—it is going somewhere.

Indeed, the Bible shows a progression of history to a definite end. It promises that the world, in which we now live with all its corruption, will one day be made into a perfect new world without sin. We read the following in the Book of Revelation.

> I heard a loud voice from the throne say, "God lives with humans! God will make his home with them, and they will be his people. God himself will be with them and be their God. He will wipe every tear from their eyes. There won't be any more death. There won't be any grief, crying, or pain, because the first things have disappeared." The one sitting on the throne said, "I am making everything new." He said, "Write this: 'These words are faithful and true'" (Revelation 21:3-5 God's Word).

Scripture speaks of a glorious future for those who believe in the Lord. There will be a new heaven and new earth where all things will be made new!

Because history has a purpose, it also means that each of us has a purpose. In fact, it is from the Bible alone that we can know our identity, our purpose, and our destiny.

WE HAVE AN IDENTITY: WHO AM I?

The Bible informs us as to who we are as human beings. Indeed, we have a genuine identity as the only part of God's creation which has been made in His image. Scripture explains what took place at the end of the sixth creative day.

> Then God said, "Let us make human beings in our image, to be like us. They will reign over the fish in the sea, the birds in the sky, the livestock, all the wild animals on the earth, and the small animals that scurry along the ground." So God created human beings in his own image. In the image of God he created them; male and female he created them (Genesis 1:26-27 NLT).

This truth, which is only revealed in Scripture, provides us with an identity. We are not a mistake—not merely here as a product of blind chance. Instead, we find that we have been made in His image.

WE HAVE A PURPOSE: WHY AM I HERE?

We have not only been created in God's image, and have an identity, we also discover from the Bible that we have a purpose for being on the earth.

Indeed, we know from Scripture that this life has genuine meaning. Once we believe in Jesus we become the salt of the earth, the light of the world. Jesus said.

> "You are the salt of the earth. But what good is salt if it has lost its flavor? Can you make it salty again? It will be thrown out and trampled underfoot as worthless. "You are the light

of the world—like a city on a hilltop that cannot be hidden. No one lights a lamp and then puts it under a basket. Instead, a lamp is placed on a stand, where it gives light to everyone in the house. In the same way, let your good deeds shine out for all to see, so that everyone will praise your heavenly Father (Matthew 5:13-16 NLT).

Believers are salt and light to this lost world.

The Bible also says that we are His ambassadors, His representatives. Paul emphasized this to the Corinthians.

So we are Christ's ambassadors; God is making his appeal through us (2 Corinthians 5:20 NLT).

Therefore, we have a purpose for living—to glorify the God of the Bible and carry out His commandments.

WE HAVE A DESTINY: WHERE AM I GOING AFTER I DIE?

Finally, there is a destiny for each and every one of us. This life is not all that there is. Long ago, a man named Job posed the question that, sooner or later, we all ask.

If someone dies, will they live again (Job 14:14 NIV).

Is there life after death? The Bible answers in the affirmative. This life is certainly not all that there is! Indeed, we have been made for eternity.

Therefore, another important reason to consider the claims of the Bible is that it reveals our destiny—a destiny for our planet as well as for us as individuals.

REASON 9: THE BIBLE TELLS US THERE IS HEAVEN FOR THOSE WHO DO BELIEVE IN JESUS

The destiny question leads us to our next reason as to why it is crucial to examine what the Bible says—there is a heaven which awaits those who believe in the God of Scripture.

HEAVEN IS WHERE JESUS IS

While the Bible reveals a number of truths about what heaven will be like, the main thing that we should realize is that heaven is where Jesus is! In fact, that is what makes it heaven. Jesus Himself promised to come back for believers.

> Jesus said to his disciples, "Don't be worried! Have faith in God and have faith in me. There are many rooms in my Father's house. I wouldn't tell you this, unless it was true. I am going there to prepare a place for each of you. After I have done this, I will come back and take you with me. Then we will be together" (John 14:1-3 CEV).

He is presently preparing a place for us. Someday Jesus will return and gather us together so that we can be with Him.

Indeed, the Apostle Paul emphasized this same truth. He wrote about what will happen when the Lord returns to take to Himself those who are His own. The result will be that each of us will be forever in His presence.

> For the Lord himself will come down from heaven, with a loud command, with the voice of the archangel and with the trumpet call of God, and the dead in Christ will rise first. After that, we who are still alive and are left will be caught up together with them in the clouds to meet the Lord in the air. And so we will be with the Lord forever. Therefore encourage one another with these words (1 Thessalonians 4:16-18 NIV).

There is, therefore, hope for those who have died "in Christ," as well as those who are alive, when the Lord comes to take His church, the true believers, out of this world. This is also called the "blessed hope." The Apostle Paul wrote elsewhere.

> While we wait for the blessed hope—the appearing of the glory of our great God and Savior, Jesus Christ (Titus 2:13 NIV).

It is truly a "blessed hope" that we have—looking forward to Christ coming for us.

In addition, we find that the Apostle Paul wrote about a personal experience he had when he was allowed to enter the presence of God. He explained it in this manner.

> I know a man in Christ who fourteen years ago was caught up to the third heaven. Whether it was in the body or out of the body I do not know—God knows. And I know that this man—whether in the body or apart from the body I do not know, but God knows—was caught up to paradise and heard inexpressible things, things that no one is permitted to tell (2 Corinthians 12:2-4 NIV).

Note that he could not even express in human terms how wonderful it was! It is above and beyond anything we could even imagine. This is our future!

REASON 10: THE BIBLE TELLS US THERE IS PUNISHMENT FOR THOSE WHO DO NOT BELIEVE IN JESUS

There is something else. For those who reject the salvation from sin offered by Jesus Christ, there is only punishment waiting. John the Apostle wrote about this. He said the following.

> Whoever believes in the Son has eternal life; whoever does not obey the Son shall not see life, but the wrath of God remains on him (John 3:36 ESV).

The Apostle Paul also testified to the future punishment of the Lord against those who have rejected Him. He wrote the following to the Thessalonians. He said.

And God will provide rest for you who are being persecuted and also for us when the Lord Jesus appears from heaven. He will come with his mighty angels, in flaming fire, bringing judgment on those who don't know God and on those who refuse to obey the Good News of our Lord Jesus. They will be punished with everlasting destruction, forever separated from the Lord and from his glorious power (2 Thessalonians 1:7-9 NLT).

Everyone will eventually acknowledge Jesus Christ is Lord. The Apostle Paul wrote the following about the past humiliation, and the ultimate exaltation, of Jesus. He said.

Have this mind among yourselves, which is yours in Christ Jesus, who, though he was in the form of God, did not count equality with God a thing to be grasped, but made himself nothing, taking the form of a servant, being born in the likeness of men. And being found in human form, he humbled himself by becoming obedient to the point of death, even death on a cross. Therefore God has highly exalted him and bestowed on him the name that is above every name, so that at the name of Jesus every knee should bow, in heaven and on earth and under the earth, and every tongue confess that Jesus Christ is Lord, to the glory of God the Father (Philippians 2:5-11 ESV).

The claim of Scripture is that the eternal destiny of every human being is based upon how they respond to the message of forgiveness through the Person of Jesus Christ. Those who reject Christ have the judgment of God waiting for them. It is only from the Scripture that we know of these claims. They are revealed nowhere else.

REASON 11: SCRIPTURE PROVIDES A STANDARD OF RIGHT AND WRONG

Where do we as humans get the concept of what is right and what is wrong? Who determines this? Is it the government that is in control at the time? Is it fifty-one percent of the population? Whoever has the biggest army? Who makes the call?

Many people do not realize that much of our modern concepts of law and order are actually based upon the Bible. Indeed, God's Law has been the basis of many of the secular concepts of right and wrong.

THE BIBLE GIVES US GOD'S STANDARDS

The Bible says that God has set standards of right and wrong behavior that human beings are to follow. He expects us to obey His commands.

After God delivered the nation of Israel from the bondage of Egypt He gave certain commandments that were to be obeyed. Scripture records it in this manner.

> Then Moses went up to God, and the Lord called to him from the mountain and said, "This is what you are to say to the descendants of Jacob and what you are to tell the people of Israel: 'You yourselves have seen what I did to Egypt, and how I carried you on eagles' wings and brought you to myself. Now if you obey me fully and keep my covenant, then out of all nations you will be my treasured possession. Although the whole earth is mine, you will be for me a kingdom of priests and a holy nation.' These are the words you are to speak to the Israelites." So Moses went back and summoned the elders of the people and set before them all the words the Lord had commanded him to speak. The people all responded together, "We will do everything the Lord has said." So Moses brought their answer back to the Lord (Exodus 19:3-8 NIV).

We find that God reminded the people of how He had miraculously delivered them from Egypt. The Lord then instructed them as to what would happen next. He would bless them as a nation—if they kept His commandments.

In fact, they would be a special people—different than all of the other nations of the earth. The people of Israel agreed with what the Lord had offered them. They would obey His commandments.

This same truth runs throughout Scripture. The Lord promises to bless His people as long as we listen to His Word and obey it.

Later we find the Lord emphasizing this particular truth. He said.

For I will honor those who honor me (1 Samuel 2:30 NET).

If we honor Him and His Word, then He will honor us. This is His promise.

HIS WORD GUIDES OUR BEHAVIOR

This standard which God has revealed to us should guide our behavior. In fact, reading, or hearing, the Word of God motivates people to change their behavior.

We find a prime example of this in the Old Testament. When the Jews returned from captivity in Babylon, the Scripture was read out loud and explained to them. We read the following in the Book of Nehemiah about what then happened.

> They read from the book of God's law, explaining it and imparting insight. Thus the people gained understanding from what was read. Then Nehemiah the governor, Ezra the priestly scribe, and the Levites who were imparting understanding to the people said to all of them, "This day is holy to the LORD your God. Do not mourn or weep." For all the people had been weeping when they heard the words of the law (Nehemiah 8:8,9 NET).

Notice that hearing the Word of God caused these people to be sorry for their past behavior, and hence, to change the way in which they were living. It was the Scripture which told them how to govern their conduct. When these people heard what God required of them, they responded.

HIS COMMANDMENTS ARE NOT DIFFICULT

We are also told in Scripture the commandments which He has given are not difficult for us to follow. John wrote

> We show our love for God by obeying his commandments,
> and they are not hard to follow (1 John 5:3 CEV).

The commandments of God should not weigh us down. God gives us His commandments to protect us and to provide for us. They are ultimately for our benefit.

Therefore, instead of rejecting what the Lord commands, we need to realize that they are given to us for the purpose of looking after us.

ALL AREAS OF HUMAN CONDUCT ARE COVERED BY SCRIPTURE

We also discover that the Bible gives commandments which cover all areas of human conduct. This includes relationships between husbands and wives, parents and children, employers and employees, and friends and enemies.

Therefore, God has provided for us the blueprint on how we are to conduct ourselves in the world. The blueprint is the Bible!

This is so important. Indeed, without God's standard of right and wrong each of us would be left to our own imaginations about what to do, what not to do, how we should behave, and how we should not behave. There could be no agreement, no consensus of opinion. Everyone would go their own way.

In fact, this is what the Bible says about each and every one of us—lost, or unbelieving humanity does not seek after God.

There is no one righteous, not even one, there is no one who understands, there is no one who seeks God. All have turned away, together they have become worthless (Romans 3:10-12 NIV).

Each of us wants to find our own way. We are not looking for Him. No, He is looking for us! We do not "find God." He is not lost—we are! He finds us!

AN IMPORTANT LESSON FROM HISTORY

In fact, this is what happened in the history of the nation Israel. During the time when Judges ruled in Israel the people continued to fall away from the Lord. The last verse in the book sums up the entire period.

> In those days there was no king in Israel. Everyone did what was right in his own eyes (Judges 21:25 ESV).

This statement basically sums up life without God. Everyone does that which seems right in their own eyes. This is what takes place when people have no ultimate standard—or ignore the standard that they know is right.

The good news is that the Lord has not left us in the dark when it comes to what is right and what is wrong. No, He has placed in the pages of Scripture the standard for our morality. This is our guidebook—our way to a successful life. We must listen to it and obey it.

REASON 12: THE BIBLE TELLS US WHAT SHOULD MOTIVATE OUR BEHAVIOR IN SERVING GOD

Christians are people who have a relationship with the true and living God through the Person of Jesus Christ. Once we believe in Christ we then should desire to be more Christlike. The Apostle Paul said that it is the will of God that we be more like Christ.

> God's will is for you to be holy (1 Thessalonians 4:3 NLT).

The meaning behind this verse is that our behavior should conform to that of the Lord Jesus. Being "holy" has the idea to be "set apart for God and for His service." This is what the will of God is for all who believe in Jesus.

John wrote something similar.

> Whoever claims to live in him must live as Jesus did (1 John 2:6 NIV).

We are to live like Jesus. However, we certainly cannot do this in our own strength. This is why the Bible commands us to be filled, or controlled, by the Holy Spirit.

Paul wrote to the Ephesians about this necessity. He contrasted being filled with the Spirit to being drunk with wine.

> Don't get drunk on wine, which leads to wild living. Instead, be filled with the Spirit (Ephesians 5:18 God's Word).

We can only please the Lord when we allow His Holy Spirit to control, or fill us. In other words, we cannot please Him if we are in control of our lives. Indeed, He is the One who must control and guide us.

THE UNIQUENESS OF THE ETHICS AND MORALS OF SCRIPTURE

While the Bible sets down a standard of morals and ethics it must be noted that these ethics and morals of the Bible are unique—they are always related to a person's belief in the existence of the God of Scripture and our relationship with Him.

Consequently, it is the *motives* that are judged rather than any outward obedience. The Bible makes this abundantly clear. The prophet Samuel declared.

> The Lord doesn't see things the way you see them. People judge by outward appearance, but the Lord looks at the heart (1 Samuel 16:7 NLT).

God looks at our attitudes—not merely on our outward behavior. In fact, we often find the people denounced for merely going through the motions in their service to God without any heartfelt desire. Jesus said.

These people honor me with their lips, but their hearts are far from me (Matthew 15:8 NIV).

This is exactly what the living God does *not* want from us! Our outward behavior should match what is in our heart. He does not merely care what we say—He cares *how* we behave and *why* we behave the way in which we do!

Therefore, the Bible gives the rules on how to behave so that we can live successfully. Yet, it also tells us the proper attitude that we should have when obeying the rules.

Consequently, the Scripture not only provides the standard for right and wrong, it tells us how we should go about following that standard.

As a result, it is not merely the outward obedience that the Lord is looking for. Instead He is looking for people who will obey Him from the heart. We read about this in the Book of Chronicles. It says.

The Lord 's eyes scan the whole world to find those whose hearts are committed to him and to strengthen them (2 Chronicles 16:9 God's Word)

This should motivate us to live godly lives. Indeed, God is looking for people to bless—those who are devoted to Him.

REASON 13: THE WORDS OF THE BIBLE MEET THE DAILY SPIRITUAL NEEDS OF BELIEVERS

Millions of Christians in the past have depended on the Bible's promises to meet their daily spiritual needs. This is still true today. Indeed, millions continue to depend upon these promises to guide their daily lives. We find that His promises are in fact true—He does meet our needs!

HE HAS PROVIDED EVERYTHING NECESSARY

The Scripture testifies that God has revealed *everything* that is necessary for us to live a godly life. Peter wrote to the believers about what Jesus Christ has provided. He said.

> God's divine power has given us everything we need for life and for godliness. This power was given to us through knowledge of the one who called us by his own glory and integrity (2 Peter 1:3 God's Word).

Notice it emphasizes that He has given us everything that we need. Everything certainly means everything!

The Apostle Paul wrote.

> My God will richly fill your every need in a glorious way through Christ Jesus (Philippians 4:19 God's Word).

We discover that God said that He would meet all our "needs," —not all of our "greeds." He provides everything that we need.

THE LORD GIVES US THE STRENGTH TO DO THIS

Paul also wrote to the Philippians about the strength that Jesus Christ provides to those who believe in Him—no matter what the circumstances may be. He put it this way.

I'm not saying this because I'm in any need. I've learned to be content in whatever situation I'm in. I know how to live in poverty or prosperity. No matter what the situation, I've learned the secret of how to live when I'm full or when I'm hungry, when I have too much or when I have too little. I can do everything through Christ who strengthens me (Philippians 4:11-13 God's Word).

The truths of the Bible give people spiritual strength to meet the challenges of each new day. This is a promise of God.

Therefore, what we find in Scripture is that God has provided the needed help for of us to get through the day. His Word is there to guide us. The psalmist wrote.

> Your word is a lamp to walk by, and a light to illumine my path (Psalm 119:105 NET).

It is His Word which lights our way.

REASON 14: SCRIPTURE PROMISES A BLESSING FOR THOSE WHO READ AND OBEY IT

There are also benefits for reading the Scripture and obeying what is contained therein. Indeed, in the Book of Revelation, we read of a "special" blessing to those who hear and obey God's Word. John wrote.

> Blessed is the one who reads the words of this prophecy aloud, and blessed are those who hear and obey the things written in it, because the time is near (Revelation 1:3 NET).

It is important that we pay close attention to this promise. The blessing is not merely for those who hear and study God's Word—the blessing is for those who hear and *obey!* Obedience is the key.

GOD PROMISES SUCCESS FOR THOSE WHO OBEY THE SCRIPTURES

For those who study, meditate upon and obey its contents, God has promised to bless them. The first Psalm promises the following.

> Blessed is the one who does not walk in step with the wicked or stand in the way that sinners take or sit in the company of mockers, but whose delight is in the law of the Lord, and who meditates on his law day and night (Psalm 1:1-2 NIV).

Those who delight in God's law will be blessed. This includes meditating or thinking about it day and night.

However, it is also assumed that those who meditate on God's Word will also obey it. Indeed, to the Hebrew mindset they did not make the distinction between studying something and obeying it! It was the same thing. Therefore, the idea is that one who studies God's Word will obey it.

THE RESULTS OF RELYING ON HIS WORD

Then the writer tells us what will be the outcome if we delight ourselves in the Lord and in His law. The Psalmist expressed it this way.

> That person is like a tree planted by streams of water, which yields its fruit in season and whose leaf does not wither—whatever they do prospers (Psalm 1:3 NIV).

What a beautiful picture! If we obey the Lord, then we will become like a fruitful tree planted next to a flowing stream. We will have a constant supply of water to allow us to bear mature fruit. Our lives will be prosperous—spiritually prosperous. We will be successful—that is, successful in God's eyes.

WE OUGHT TO CONTINUALLY STUDY AND OBEY

God elsewhere commands believers to study His written Word, meditate upon it, and obey it. The Lord told Joshua the necessity of doing this. He said.

> Keep this Book of the Law always on your lips; meditate on it day and night, so that you may be careful to do everything written in it. Then you will be prosperous and successful (Joshua 1:8 NIV).

Notice that as one studies God's Word they are to act in accordance with it. Consequently, studying and understanding what we are studying, is not enough—one must put into practice what the Word of God teaches.

WE LIVE OUR LIVES BY GOD'S WORD

This corresponds with what Jesus said. He made it clear that we are to live by God's Word. In one of His temptations with the devil, Jesus responded as follows.

> But he [Jesus] answered, "It is written, 'One does not live by bread alone, but by every word that comes from the mouth of God'" (Matthew 4:4).

We cannot exist on physical food alone. To truly live in this world in the way we were meant to live, we also must live on spiritual food. Physical food will keep us alive physically but spiritual food is necessary for us to live spiritually.

In fact, the Book of Deuteronomy says that God's words are "the words of life." Moses wrote the following to the children of Israel.

> They are not just idle words for you—they are your life. By them you will live long in the land you are crossing the Jordan to possess (Deuteronomy 32:47 NIV).

The words of God are the words of life! Therefore, it is essential that we put into practice the things which God has commanded us.

GOD DELIGHTS IN THOSE WHO TREMBLE AT HIS WORD

The Bible also says God delights in those who humbly tremble at His Word. The Lord said the following to the prophet Isaiah.

> Has not my hand made all these things, and so they came into being?" declares the Lord. "These are the ones I look on with favor: those who are humble and contrite in spirit, and who tremble at my word" (Isaiah 66:2 NIV).

To have God delight in us we must have a humble heart when approaching Him and His Word.

HE REJOICES OVER US WITH SINGING!

Interestingly, we are told that God takes great delight over us by actually singing! The prophet Zephaniah wrote about the future attitude of the Lord toward the nation Israel when they humbly return to Him in faith.

> The LORD your God is with you, the Mighty Warrior who saves. He will take great delight in you; in his love he will no longer rebuke you, but will rejoice over you with singing (Zephaniah 3:17 NIV).

Truly this is a humbling thought! The living God will rejoice over us with singing—when we trust and obey Him.

In the same manner, Moses wrote to the children of Israel about the importance of following the commands of the Lord with all their heart.

> The Lord your God will make you abundantly prosperous in all the work of your hand, in the fruit of your womb and in the fruit of your cattle and in the fruit of your ground. For the Lord will again take delight in prospering you, as he took delight in your fathers, when you obey the voice of the Lord your God, to keep his commandments and his statutes that are written in this Book of the Law, when you turn to the Lord your God with all your heart and with all your soul (Deuteronomy 30:9,10 NIV).

Thus, it is of utmost importance that we have a proper attitude toward the Bible. It is not merely a record of the history of Israel, or the New Testament church—it is God's divinely inspired communication with the human race. We are to read it, study it, and obey it.

Furthermore, it is crucial that we have the right attitude when we obey what is written in the Scripture. It is not enough merely to go through the motions of obeying what is commanded. The Bible says that God is looking at our attitude. This is something that we should never forget.

REASON 15: THE BIBLE HAS INFLUENCED HUMANITY LIKE NO OTHER BOOK IN HISTORY

After having looked at the previous fourteen reasons as to why it is important to consider the claims of the Bible, the last point we will look at should not be a surprise to us. Indeed, if the Bible is what it claims to be, then we should expect that it would have had an influence like no other book in history.

And this is exactly the case. Among other reasons, it is important that we should know and understand the contents of the Bible because of the influence which it has had on the world.

While the Bible is one of the oldest books which is still being published, it remains the world's best-seller. No other book even comes close. In fact, over one hundred million copies of the Bible, or parts of it, are printed each year. The Scriptures have been translated into over one thousand languages and dialects!

THE BIBLE HAS A HAD A ONE-OF-A-KIND INFLUENCE

No other writing, ancient or modern, has had nearly the influence on the human race as has the Bible. Indeed, every day the message of the Bible continues to changes lives in all parts of the world, and at every level of society. The Bible is truly one of a kind—it has no equal.

There is certainly a reason for this. It is not because of any hype or slick marketing program. No, the Bible remains the world's best-seller because it contains the "words of eternal life."

When Jesus was speaking to the multitudes there were many who walked away from him. Jesus asked His disciples if they were going to leave also. Simon Peter answered for them.

> From this time many of his disciples turned back and no longer followed him. "You do not want to leave too, do you?" Jesus asked the Twelve. Simon Peter answered him, "Lord,

to whom shall we go? You have the words of eternal life" (John 6:66-68 NIV).

Their answer was clear—there is nowhere else to go! Only Jesus has the words of eternal life. These words are contained in His Word, the Bible.

IT IS THE ONLY BOOK THAT HAS ANSWERS

Again we want to stress that it is the Bible, and the Bible alone, that contains the answers to our deepest questions. Furthermore, it informs us of the way we should live our lives, as well as how we can have our deepest needs met.

CONCLUSION: IT IS IMPORTANT THAT WE READ AND STUDY THE BIBLE

A book that has the credentials such as these should be examined by all serious people. The Bible claims to be God's communication to humanity—it is His way of talking to us.

Therefore, it is crucial that we understand the Bible as a personal correspondence between the Creator and His creation. In the Bible, God communicated the fact that He wants to establish a relationship between Himself and with each individual. This is the main message of Scripture.

SUMMARY TO QUESTION 2
IS IT IMPORTANT TO CONSIDER THE CLAIMS OF THE BIBLE? (15 REASONS WHY)

The Bible is the most important book that has ever been written—it claims to be the very Word of God. Indeed, all Christian doctrine, or teaching, is based upon what the Bible says. It speaks with final authority on all matters.

Furthermore, the Bible offers answers to life's basic questions. These include the existence and nature of God, the identity and purpose of humankind, the story of human history, the meaning of history, and scientific questions about the nature of the universe. It was specifically written to cause people to believe in Jesus Christ.

In addition, it predicts judgment, and then punishment, for those who do not believe in Jesus. The Bible also provides a basis of right and wrong, a standard for how to live successfully, as well as a practical guide for daily needs. In short, it is the most important Book that has ever been, or will ever be, written.

This is why the Bible continues to be the world's best-seller. It wields its influence every day to all parts of the globe. Therefore, it is of crucial importance that people take time to read and study the Scriptures.

What Special Terms Does the Bible Use to Describe Itself?

One of the ways in which Scripture claims to be God's Word is in the number of special terms it uses in describing itself. They include the following.

THE SCRIPTURE (SCRIPTURES) THE WRITINGS

The New Testament applied the term "the writings" to the books of the Old Testament. The term "Scripture" comes from the Greek word graphe meaning, "a writing," or "that which is written." The noun form of the word occurs about fifty times in the New Testament, and it is used mostly of the collection of sacred writings—the Old Testament.

THE GREEK WORD GRAPHE [SCRIPTURE] IS USED IN THE SINGULAR AND THE PLURAL WHEN REFERRING TO THE OLD TESTAMENT

Both the singular and the plural form of *graphe* are used to describe the sacred writings. In Matthew's gospel, the plural form of *graphe* is used.

We find this term used when Jesus confronted those who rejected His claim to be the promised Messiah. In doing so, He quoted the Scripture.

> Jesus said to them, "Have you never read in the Scriptures." 'The stone that the builders rejected has become the cornerstone; this was the Lord's doing, and it is marvelous in our eyes' (Matthew 21:42 ESV).

The parallel passage in Mark has the singular form of this Greek word. Jesus said.

> Have you not even read this Scripture: "The stone which the builders rejected has become the chief cornerstone" (Mark 12:10 NKJV).

Therefore, both the singular, as well as the plural form of *graphe* are used to refer to the written Word of God.

THE WORD TRANSLATED SCRIPTURE CAN REFER TO ONE SPECIFIC PASSAGE

The word Scripture is sometimes used of a specific passage in the sacred writings. After Jesus had read a passage from the scroll of Isaiah, He put the scroll down. He then made a comment that astonished those who were in attendance. Luke writes.

> Then he [Jesus] began to tell them, "Today this scripture has been fulfilled even as you heard it being read" (Luke 4:21 NET).

In this case, the term "Scripture" refers to one specific passage in the sacred writings.

THE WORD SCRIPTURE IS ALSO USED OF THE WORDS OF JESUS

The term "Scripture" is even used of specific New Testament portions. In 1 Timothy 5:18, Paul directly quoted the words of Christ that are recorded in Luke 10:7 and called the words "Scripture."

> For Scripture says, "Do not muzzle an ox while it is treading out the grain," and "The worker deserves his wages" (1 Timothy 5:18 NIV).

The New Living Translation puts it this way.

For the Scripture says, "Do not keep an ox from eating as it treads out the grain." And in another place, "Those who work deserve their pay!" (1 Timothy 5:18 NLT).

The phrase, "the worker deserves his wages," or "those who work deserve their pay" is something that Luke recorded Jesus saying to His disciples. Jesus said.

Stay there, eating and drinking whatever they give you, for the worker deserves his wages. Do not move around from house to house (Luke 10:7 NIV).

This is the earliest instance of Jesus' words being specifically cited as Scripture. This citation is from the New Testament itself.

PAUL'S WRITINGS ARE CALLED SCRIPTURE

In 2 Peter 3:16, Peter specifically refers to Paul's writings as Scripture. He wrote the following to the believers.

And count the patience of our Lord as salvation, just as our beloved brother Paul also wrote to you according to the wisdom given him, as he does in all his letters when he speaks in them of these matters. There are some things in them that are hard to understand, which the ignorant and unstable twist to their own destruction, as they do the other Scriptures (2 Peter 3:15,16 ESV).

The words "other Scriptures," or "other parts of Scripture," would refer to the Old Testament, as well as that portion of the New Testament that had been written at that time. The writings of Paul were of the same authority as these other sacred writings.

THE PHRASE "IT IS WRITTEN" IS USED TO REFER TO HOLY SCRIPTURE

The verb form of the Greek word *graphe* is used about ninety times. It is often found in a form meaning, "It is written." For example, we read the following in Matthew's gospel.

Then Jesus told him, "Go away, Satan! For it is written: Worship the Lord your God, and serve only Him" (Matthew 4:10 HCSB).

Therefore, we find the word translated as "Scripture" or "Scriptures" used in a number of different ways to designate the holy writings.

THE HOLY SCRIPTURES (THE HOLY WRITINGS)

Twice we find the Old Testament called the "holy Scriptures," the "holy writings," or the "sacred writings." When Paul wrote to Timothy, he reminded him how the sacred Scripture had been a part of his life since the beginning. He said.

> And how from childhood you have been acquainted with the sacred writings which are able to make you wise for salvation through faith in Christ Jesus (2 Timothy 3:15 ESV).

In this instance, Paul used the Greek word *gramma* to refer to the Scriptures.

Paul also used the word *gramma* when he wrote to the church at Rome. He introduced the letter in the following manner.

> Paul, a slave of Christ Jesus, called as an apostle and singled out for God's good news—which He promised long ago through His prophets in the Holy Scriptures (Romans 1:1,2 HCSB).

The consistent testimony is that the Scriptures are holy and sacred writings. This has the idea that these writings are set apart for a special purpose.

THE WORD OF GOD

"The Word of God" is a title that is used in both Testaments to speak of the sacred writings. This expression emphasizes the nature of the Bible as the revelation of God to humanity in written form. In Matthew, this expression is used specifically of the Law of Moses. Jesus rebuked the religious leaders for their dishonoring of the "Word of God." The Bible says.

> And why do you break God's commandment because of your tradition? For God said: Honor your father and your mother; and, the one who speaks evil of father or mother must be put to death. But you say, 'Whoever tells his father or mother, "Whatever benefit you might have received from me is a gift committed to the temple"—he does not have to honor his father.' In this way, you have revoked God's word because of your tradition. Hypocrites! (Matthew 15:3-6 HCSB).

In Mark 7:13, the phrase, "the Word of God" is also used of Moses' command regarding the honoring of a person's father and mother. Jesus said.

> Thus you nullify the word of God by your tradition that you have handed down. And you do many things like this (Mark 7:13 NET).

In John 10:35, Jesus used the phrase "the Word of God" to refer to the entire Old Testament. He said.

> If He called them gods, to whom the word of God came (and the Scripture cannot be broken), do you say of Him whom the Father sanctified and sent into the world, 'You are blaspheming,' because I said, 'I am the Son of God'? (John 10:35,36 NKJV).

Thus, the sacred writings are considered to be the very Word of God.

THE WORD OF THE LORD

In various portions of the Bible, God's Word is referred to as the "Word of the Lord." Peter, quoting the prophet Isaiah, wrote the following.

> For, "All men are like grass, and all their glory is like the flowers of the field; the grass withers and the flowers fall, but the word of the Lord stands forever" (1 Peter 1:24,25 NIV).

The word translated "Lord" refers to the divine name for God—Yahweh or Jehovah. Thus, the Scriptures are the Word of Yahweh or Jehovah Himself.

A DEPENDABLE BOOK (BOOK OF TRUTH)

In Daniel, we find the written Word called a "dependable book" or a "book of truth." An angelic messenger approached Daniel and said the following.

> However, I will first tell you what is written in a dependable book (Daniel 10:21 NET).

Some translations see the words "dependable book" as a title, "The Book of Truth." The New International Version translates this verse in this manner.

> But first I will tell you what is written in the Book of Truth (Daniel 10:21 NIV).

The New King James Version also sees it as a title, but translates it as "The Scripture of Truth." It reads as follows.

> But I will tell you what is noted in the Scripture of Truth (Daniel 10:21 NKJV).

The New Revised Standard Version has a similar translation to these three English versions but does not capitalize the words as a title.

> But I am to tell you what is inscribed in the book of truth (Daniel 10:21 NRSV).

The English Standard Version translates it in a similar way as the New Revised Standard Version. It says the following.

But I will tell you what is inscribed in the book of truth (Daniel 10:21 ESV).

The point is that the testimony of Scripture is entirely trustworthy. The ultimate author of the Bible, God, cannot lie. Therefore, His Word is entirely dependable!

THE SACRED BOOKS (THE SACRED SCROLLS)

Daniel the prophet used the term, "the sacred books" or the "sacred scrolls" to refer to the holy writings. He wrote the following.

> In the first year of his reign I, Daniel, came to understand from the sacred books that, according to the word of the LORD disclosed to the prophet Jeremiah, the years for the fulfilling of the reproach of Jerusalem were seventy in number (Daniel 9:2 NET).

The Apostle Paul also used the term "scrolls" to refer to the sacred writings. He wrote the following to Timothy.

> When you come, bring with you the cloak I left in Troas with Carpas and the scrolls, especially the parchment ones (2 Timothy 4:13 NET).

While Paul may have been referring to the Old Testament, it is possible that his own writings were meant. Indeed, in his earliest writing (1 Thessalonians) he claimed that his message was not merely his own words but actually the word of God.

> We also constantly give thanks to God for this, that when you received the word of God that you heard from us, you accepted it not as a human word but as what it really is, God's word, which is also at work in you believers (1 Thessalonians 2:13 NRSV).

However, one must be careful in assuming that any reference in the Bible to a book or books must, of necessity, refer to the sacred Scripture. Depending upon the context, the Greek word translated "book" or "scroll" can also refer to a book of magic. We find an example of this in the Book of Acts.

> And a number of those who had practiced magic arts brought their books together and burned them in the sight of all. And they counted the value of them and found it came to fifty thousand pieces of silver (Acts 19:19 ESV).

Therefore, the Scripture uses the terms "book" and "books" in a number of different ways—including sacred books.

THE LAW

A term used in the New Testament for the Old Testament Scripture is, "the Law." The expression often refers to the entire Old Testament while at other times it is speaking the Law of Moses—the first five books of the Bible. In John 12:34, for example, we find it referring to the entire Old Testament. It says.

> The crowd answered him, "We have heard from the law that the Messiah remains forever. How can you say that the Son of Man must be lifted up? Who is this Son of Man?" (John 12:34 NRSV).

There is nothing in the Law of Moses, the first five books of Scripture, which says the Christ will live forever. In this context "the Law" is used of the entire Old Testament. The following verses teach that Christ will live forever.

> The Lord has sworn an oath and will not take it back: "Forever, You are a priest like Melchizedek (Psalm 110:4 HCSB).

Isaiah the prophet predicted a number of things that would be true about the coming Messiah, or Christ. He wrote.

> His dominion will be vast and he will bring immeasurable prosperity. He will rule on David's throne and over David's kingdom, establishing it and strengthening it by promoting justice and fairness, from this time forward and forevermore. The LORD's intense devotion to his people will accomplish this (Isaiah 9:7 NET).

Therefore, the term "Law" can refer have a narrow meaning, the Law of Moses, or a much wider meaning—the entire Old Testament.

THE LAW AND THE PROPHETS

Another New Testament expression used for the entire Old Testament is the "Law and the Prophets." It looks at the Old Testament from the standpoint of how it was divided at that time. The Apostle Paul used this expression when wrote to the church at Rome.

> But now, apart from law, the righteousness of God has been disclosed, and is attested by the law and the prophets (Romans 3:21 NRSV).

This was a common designation for the Old Testament.

MOSES AND THE PROPHETS

The Old Testament is also called "Moses and the prophets." In the story that Jesus told of the rich man and Lazarus, both of them had died. In the narrative, we find Abraham speaking to the rich man in the next world.

> Abraham replied, "They have Moses and the prophets; they should listen to them" (Luke 16:29 NRSV).

Here, Moses is another term for "the Law."

THE LAW, THE PROPHETS, AND THE PSALMS

Jesus spoke of a threefold division of the Old Testament—the Law, the Prophets, and the Psalms. In Luke's gospel, we read.

> Then he [Jesus] said to them, "These are my words that I spoke to you while I was still with you—that everything written about me in the law of Moses, the prophets, and the psalms must be fulfilled" (Luke 24:44 NRSV).

In this context, the term "psalms" may refer to the wisdom books of the Old Testament. This would include the Book of Psalms, the Book of Proverbs and the Book of Job. However, there is no clear evidence that these books were divided this way at this time in history. Therefore, this reference of Jesus may be only referring to the Book of Psalms.

THE ORACLES OF GOD (LIVING ORACLES)

Another term for the holy writings is the Greek word *logion*. This is a diminutive form of the Greek word *logos* and means "an oracle, divine response, or utterance." It is used of the sacred writings in Romans 3:2 and Acts 7:38. Paul wrote.

> What advantage then has the Jew, or what is the profit of circumcision? Much in every way! Chiefly because to them were committed the oracles of God (Romans 3:1,2 NKJV).

In the Book of Acts, the martyr Stephen referred to these words as "living oracles." In speaking to a hostile crowd, he said.

> This is the man who was in the congregation in the wilderness with the angel who spoke to him at Mount Sinai, and with our ancestors, and he received living oracles to give to you (Acts 7:38 NET).

The Word of God is living—it has the power to change lives.

THE COVENANT (TESTAMENT)

The word "covenant," or "testament," is also used for the sacred Scripture. The Greek word *diatheke* translated "testament," means, "covenant, contract, or will." It is used to distinguish between the Old and New Covenants—the Old Testament and the New Testament. The Apostle Paul wrote about the Jews reading the old covenant.

> But their minds were hardened. For to this day, when they read the old covenant, that same veil remains unlifted, because only through Christ is it taken away (2 Corinthians 3:14 ESV).

The first coming of Jesus Christ explains the meaning of the Old Covenant, as well as explaining its promises.

THE USE OF THE TERMS BOOK, AND THE BOOKS, AFTER BIBLICAL TIMES

After the New Testament era, the terms "book" and "books" began to be used to refer to the collection of sacred writings—the Old and New Testament. The change came about as believers viewed the two testaments as one unified utterance of God. Today, the most popular term to describe God's Word is the term Bible. This emphasizes that the Scripture is ultimately one Book.

To sum up, there are a number of terms that the Bible uses to describe itself. It is clear from these terms that this "Book" should be regard as God's Holy Word.

SUMMARY TO QUESTION 3
WHAT SPECIAL TERMS DOES THE BIBLE USE TO DESCRIBE ITSELF?

Twelve biblical expressions—Scripture, the Holy Scripture, the Word of God, the Word of the Lord, the Book of Truth, the sacred Books, the Law, the Law and the Prophets, the Law, the Prophets, and the Psalms, Moses and the Prophets, the Oracles of God, and Covenant—are the designations used for the collection of writings that were considered sacred by the writers of the Bible. This demonstrates the attitude that was taken toward these books—they are the Word of God.

Both testaments claim to record the words and deeds of God. The New Testament uses terms such as "Scripture," "Oracles" and "Testament" when referring to the Old Testament. Each of these terms shows that the writings were considered to be sacred, or divinely inspired. It is, therefore, the claim of the Bible that it is the revealed Word of God.

Why Are the Two Divisions of the Bible Called the Old and New Testament?

The Bible is divided into two testaments—the Old and the New "Testament." What is the purpose for the division? Why are they called "testaments?"

A TESTAMENT IS A COVENANT OR AGREEMENT

Testament is an old English word that means, "covenant," or "agreement between two parties." It was derived from the Latin *testamentum*. This term was used to translate the Greek and Hebrew words for covenant—*berit* in Hebrew and *diatheke* in Greek. Hence the Old and New Covenants became the Old and New Testaments. This is the ancient meaning of the term.

However, the two parts of Scripture are not "testaments" in the modern sense of the word—a last will and testament. Rather, the term speaks of an agreement, covenant, or contract. Consequently, it is unfortunate that the English word "testament" is still used to describe the Old and New Covenants that God has made with His people.

Before Jesus came to the earth there was only one group of sacred writings—there was no "Old" Testament. However, after it was recognized that God had given further sacred writings to humanity, believers began to distinguish between the two groups of written Scripture.

THERE ARE A NUMBER OF COVENANTS RECORDED IN THE OLD TESTAMENT

In the Bible, the word covenant usually has the idea of an agreement between two parties where one party is superior to the other—it is not an agreement between equals. The superior party makes a covenant in which he agrees to give certain things to the inferior party. This is the idea behind the agreements that God has made with the human race.

One of the central themes of the Old Testament is the idea of a covenant, or agreement, between God and humankind. The Bible lists a number of covenants that God instituted. They include the following.

1. THE COVENANT GOD MADE WITH ADAM AND EVE

The first covenant in Scripture is the one God made with Adam and Eve. The Bible records it in the following manner.

> The LORD God took the man and placed him in the orchard in Eden to care for and maintain it. Then the LORD God commanded the man, "You may freely eat fruit from every tree of the orchard, but you must not eat from the tree of the knowledge of good and evil, for when you eat from it you will surely die" (Genesis 2:15-17 NET).

As long as Adam and Eve obeyed God, they would live in paradise—without any sin or evil in their lives. When Adam and Eve broke their part of the covenant, sin entered into the world.

2. THE COVENANT GOD MADE WITH NOAH

After the Flood, God made a covenant or agreement with Noah. The Lord said to him.

> But I will establish My covenant with you; and you shall go into the ark—you, your sons, your wife, and your sons' wives with you (Genesis 6:18 NKJV).

The New English Translation translates the verse this way.

> But I will confirm my covenant with you. You will enter the
> ark—you, your sons, your wife, and your sons' wives with
> you (Genesis 6:18 NET).

In this covenant with Noah, God promised that He would never destroy the earth again by means of a flood. As a token of the covenant, the Lord gave an external sign—the sign of the rainbow.

3. THE COVENANT GOD MADE WITH ABRAHAM

God made a covenant with a man named Abram (his name was later changed to Abraham). In this agreement, He promised to bless Abraham's descendants. The Bible records what happened.

> Now the LORD said to Abram, "Go out from your country,
> your relatives, and your father's household to the land that
> I will show you. Then I will make you into a great nation,
> and I will bless you, and I will make your name great, in
> order that you might be a prime example of divine bless-
> ing. I will bless those who bless you, but the one who treats
> you lightly I must curse, and all the families of the earth
> will pronounce blessings on one another using your name"
> (Genesis 12:1-3 NET).

This was the beginning of what would later become the nation of Israel. The token of the covenant with the descendants of Abraham was the circumcision of the male children. This was the external sign that these people belonged to the Lord.

4. THE COVENANT GOD MADE WITH MOSES

The Old Testament, or Old Covenant, derives its name from the agreement that God made with the nation of Israel at Mt. Sinai. The Bible explains it as follows.

> On the third new moon after the people of Israel had gone out of the land of Egypt, on that day they came into the wilderness of Sinai. They set out from Rephidim and came into the wilderness of Sinai, and they encamped in the wilderness. There Israel encamped before the mountain, while Moses went up to God. The Lord called to him out of the mountain, saying, "Thus you shall say to the house of Jacob, and tell the people of Israel: You yourselves have seen what I did to the Egyptians, and how I bore you on eagles' wings and brought you to myself. Now therefore, if you will indeed obey my voice and keep my covenant, you shall be my treasured possession among all peoples, for all the earth is mine; and you shall be to me a kingdom of priests and a holy nation. These are the words that you shall speak to the people of Israel" (Exodus 19:1-6 ESV).

God emphasized that He would have a personal relationship with His people. He said.

> And I will walk among you and will be your God, and you shall be my people (Leviticus 26:12 ESV).

Israel was the only nation that would have a special relationship with the Lord—they were His chosen people. They were to worship Him exclusively.

5. THE COVENANT GOD MADE WITH DAVID

Later in the history of Israel, God made a covenant with King David. The Bible records it as follows.

> When your days are fulfilled and you lie down with your fathers, I will raise up your offspring after you, who shall come from your body, and I will establish his kingdom. He shall build a house for my name, and I will establish the throne of his kingdom forever. I will be to him a father, and

he shall be to me a son. When he commits iniquity, I will discipline him with the rod of men, with the stripes of the sons of men, but my steadfast love will not depart from him, as I took it from Saul, whom I put away from before you. And your house and your kingdom shall be made sure forever before me. Your throne shall be established forever. In accordance with all these words, and in accordance with all this vision, Nathan spoke to David (2 Samuel 7:12-17 ESV).

In this covenant, God promised David that one of his descendants would build a house for the Lord and rule forever as king over the nation Israel. The initial fulfillment of this promise was found in David's son, Solomon. He is the one who built the temple for the Lord, and ruled over the nation, but he certainly did not rule forever.

Indeed, there are promises listed in this passage that go beyond that which was fulfilled by Solomon. The agreement God made with David found its ultimate fulfillment in Jesus. The Bible records the visit of the angel Gabriel to the virgin Mary who explained how this covenant is fulfilled in Jesus. The Bible says.

In the sixth month the angel Gabriel was sent by God to a town in Galilee called Nazareth, to a virgin engaged to a man whose name was Joseph, of the house of David. The virgin's name was Mary. And he came to her and said, "Greetings, favored one! The Lord is with you." But she was much perplexed by his words and pondered what sort of greeting this might be. The angel said to her, "Do not be afraid, Mary, for you have found favor with God. And now, you will conceive in your womb and bear a son, and you will name him Jesus. He will be great, and will be called the Son of the Most High, and the Lord God will give to him the throne of his ancestor David. He will reign over the house of Jacob forever, and of his kingdom there will be no end" (Luke 1:26-33 NRSV).

Jesus is the ultimate fulfillment of the promise to David that one of his descendants would rule forever. Jesus, the Son of David, will rule the world from David's throne when He comes again.

This brings up an important distinction that we find in the Old Testament, or Old Covenant. There were two lines of teaching in the Old Testament about the Promised Deliverer or Messiah. One emphasis was that David's son, the Messiah, would restore humanity to a right relationship with God. This would occur by Him being an offering or sacrifice for sin.

Another line of teaching had David's son ruling over the nations. Israel is restored as God's chosen people with David's son ruling as king.

Each of these purposes is seen in prophetic pictures in the Old Testament. The New Testament says part one was fulfilled at the First Coming of Christ, while part two will be fulfilled at His Second Coming.

A NEW COVENANT IS PROMISED

In the Book of Jeremiah we find a new covenant, or a new contract, promised to the people of God. It says.

> "The day will come," says the LORD, "when I will make a new covenant with the people of Israel and Judah. This covenant will not be like the one I made with their ancestors when I took them by the hand and brought them out of the land of Egypt. They broke that covenant, though I loved them as a husband loves his wife," says the LORD. "But this is the new covenant I will make with the people of Israel on that day," says the LORD. "I will put my laws in their minds, and I will write them on their hearts. I will be their God, and they will be my people" (Jeremiah 31:31-33 NLT).

The new covenant promised that the Law of God would be written on the hearts of the people. The Lord promised that this new covenant would take the place of the old one—making the old covenant unnecessary.

THE NEW COVENANT IS INSTITUTED BY JESUS CHRIST

Jesus instituted the New Covenant, or the New Contract, on the night in which He was betrayed. The Gospel of Matthew records what took place. It says.

> Now as they were eating, Jesus took bread, and after blessing it broke it and gave it to the disciples, and said, "Take, eat; this is my body." And he took a cup, and when he had given thanks he gave it to them, saying, "Drink of it, all of you, for this is my blood of the covenant, which is poured out for many for the forgiveness of sins" (Matthew 26:26-28 ESV).

The Apostle Paul wrote to the Corinthians about the new covenant. He explained it in this manner.

> Not that we are competent in ourselves to claim anything for ourselves, but our competence comes from God. He has made us competent as ministers of a new covenant—not of the letter but of the Spirit; for the letter kills, but the Spirit gives life (2 Corinthians 3:5,6 NIV).

Believers today are ministers of a new covenant.

SOME IMPORTANT POINTS ABOUT THE NEW COVENANT

Five points need to be made about the "New Covenant." They are as follows.

1. THE NEW COVENANT WAS INSTITUTED BY THE DEATH OF JESUS CHRIST

The new covenant is based upon the death of Jesus Christ on the cross of Calvary. Paul wrote.

> In the same way, after supper He also took the cup and said, "This cup is the new covenant established by My blood. Do this, as often as you drink it, in remembrance of Me (1 Corinthians 11:25 HCSB).

The New Living Translation renders this verse as follows.

> In the same way, he took the cup of wine after supper, saying, "This cup is the new covenant between God and you, sealed by the shedding of my blood. Do this in remembrance of me as often as you drink it" (1 Corinthians 11:25 NLT).

Jesus' death brought about this new covenant relationship between God and His people. The bread and the wine are memorials of this New Covenant. The wine represents the blood of the covenant. The Bible records Jesus saying.

> "This is my blood of the covenant, which is poured out for many," he said to them (Mark 14:24 NIV).

This would remind the people of the words of Moses when God made a covenant with the children of Israel at Mt. Sinai. The Bible says.

> So Moses took the blood and splashed it on the people and said, "This is the blood of the covenant that the Lord has made with you in accordance with all these words" (Exodus 24:8 NET).

Jesus' blood is the token of the New Covenant.

2. GOD NOW DEALS EXCLUSIVELY WITH HUMANITY THROUGH THE NEW COVENANT

The major theme of the New Testament is how God now deals with humanity through the new covenant. In the New Testament, the Old Testament writings are called the "old covenant." Paul wrote.

We are not like Moses, who used to put a veil over his face so that the Israelites could not stare at the the end of what was fading away, but their minds were closed. For to this day, at the reading of the old covenant, the same veil remains; it is not lifted, because it is set aside only in Christ (2 Corinthians 3:13,14 HCSB).

Jesus' death on the cross put an end to the sacrificial system. In the Old Covenant, with the old system, the sin problem was dealt with through animal sacrifices. These sacrifices are no longer necessary.

3. THE OLD COVENANT IS NOW OBSOLETE

Because God is now dealing with humanity on the basis of the "new covenant," the first covenant is now obsolete and outdated. The writer to the Hebrews stated.

By calling this covenant "new," he has made the first one obsolete; and what is obsolete and outdated will soon disappear (Hebrews 8:13 NIV).

We also read in Hebrews about how the first covenant has been cancelled.

Then he added, "Look, I have come to do your will." He cancels the first covenant in order to establish the second (Hebrews 10:9 NLT).

God is now dealing with humanity through a New Covenant—the one that was instituted by the death of Jesus Christ. Everyone who participates in the New Covenant must personally believe that Jesus Christ died on the cross for their sins, and then rose from the dead. This is the only way that they can have a personal relationship with God.

4. THE OLD COVENANT AND THE NEW COVENANT GAVE RISE TO A GROUP OF HOLY WRITINGS

There is another thing that should be mentioned about the Old Covenant and the New Covenant. Each covenant launched a great spiritual work of the Lord. The Old Covenant was God's unique workings with the nation Israel. The New Covenant extends to all people throughout the world.

Furthermore, these covenants gave rise to a body of sacred literature. Once each covenant was instituted, a number of sacred writings were given by God to explain the meaning of the covenant.

Our Old Testament consists of the books of the Old Covenant while the New Testament books are writings that are based upon the new covenant that God has made with humanity.

5. THE LAW OF GOD IS PRESENTLY IN THE HEARTS OF THE PEOPLE

The writer to the Hebrews said that God would put the law into the hearts of people under the new covenant. He wrote.

> And the Holy Spirit also testifies that this is so. First he says, "This is the new covenant I will make with my people on that day, says the Lord: I will put my laws in their hearts so they will understand them, and I will write them on their minds so they will obey them." Then he adds, "I will never again remember their sins and lawless deeds" (Hebrews 10:15-17 NLT).

The wonderful promise of God made possible through the death of Jesus, is that God's law in now placed in the hearts of those who believe in Him. Under the New Covenant, God gives His people the ability to carry out the terms of the covenant. The token of this covenant is the Holy Spirit who lives inside each believer. He empowers believers to follow Christ and to obey the terms of the New Covenant.

As we examine the various agreements that God has made with humanity, we find that God has always kept His part of the agreement. Unfortunately, the same thing cannot be said about the response of humans. We have miserably failed. This is why a Savior is desperately needed.

SUMMARY TO QUESTION 4
WHY ARE THE TWO DIVISIONS OF THE BIBLE CALLED THE OLD AND NEW TESTAMENT?

The Bible is divided into two testaments, or covenants—the old and the new. Testament is not the best word to describe these parts of Scripture. They are not part of a last will or testament, but rather an agreement, or contract that God has made with His people.

In the Bible, the covenant is usually seen as an agreement between a superior and one who is inferior—it is not an agreement between equals. The superior member grants certain rights and privileges to the inferior member. This is illustrated by the various covenants that God has made with His people.

The Bible speaks of different agreements that God made with humanity. Indeed, the entire flow of biblical history, the unfolding drama of God's redemption of the human race, is based upon the covenants that God has made with humankind.

In the Bible, we find covenants made with Adam, Noah, Abraham, Moses, and David. Certain of the covenants came with visible signs. For example, God gave Noah the sign of the rainbow as a reminder of His agreement with Noah—He would never again destroy humanity with a Flood. The descendants of Abraham were to be circumcised to demonstrate their willingness to fulfill their covenant.

Through the prophet Jeremiah, God also promised a new covenant. Jesus Himself is the One who instituted the new covenant. His broken body, His shed blood, are the tokens of the New Covenant. The Old Testament, or Old Covenant, is now obsolete.

Both covenants have given rise to a new spiritual movement as well as to a body of sacred literature—the Old and New Testament. Each of these testaments explains the terms of the covenant.

The good news is that the law of God is now written on the hearts of the people of the New Covenant—those who believe in Him. God has given His Holy Spirit as a token, or sign, or this New Covenant. This gives Christians the ability, as well as the desire, to carry out the terms of the covenant.

God has kept His part of the bargain in all of these covenants. However, humanity miserably failed to keep their part. This is why a Savior is desperately needed.

What Value Does the Old Testament Have?

To many people, the Old Testament is irrelevant today. They consider only the New Testament to have any real value. However, there are a number of reasons as to why the Old Testament is extremely important to study. They include the following.

IT WAS THE BIBLE OF JESUS, THE APOSTLES, AND FIRST-CENTURY JEWS

At the time of Jesus, there was no such thing as a "new" testament. The Hebrew Scriptures were the only divine writings that God had revealed to humanity. It revealed the words and the works of the one true God throughout history, as well as the response of the people to God's revelation of Himself. God had made Himself known to humanity through His miraculous deeds which were explained and interpreted by His divinely chosen spokesmen—the prophets. They explained the meaning of the various acts of mercy and judgment. Consequently, the books of the Old Testament were the Bible for Jesus, His apostles, and other first-century Jews.

Because of the importance of the Hebrew Scripture, Jesus assured His listeners that He had not come to abolish what had been written. He said.

> Do not think that I have come to abolish the Law or the Prophets; I have not come to abolish them but to fulfill

> them. For truly, I say to you, until heaven and earth pass
> away, not an iota, not a dot, will pass from the Law until all
> is accomplished (Matthew 5:17-18 ESV).

He held the Scriptures in the highest regard. On His way to Jerusalem
to die for the sins of the world, Jesus said the following to His disciples
about the Scriptures.

> Then He took the Twelve aside and told them, "Listen! We
> are going up to Jerusalem. Everything that is written through
> the prophets about the Son of Man will be accomplished"
> (Luke 18:31 HCSB).

Things that are important to Jesus should be important to us. Since the
Old Testament was His Bible, it should cause us to have the utmost
reverence and respect for it.

THE OLD TESTAMENT WAS IMPORTANT TO PAUL

The same is true of Saul of Tarsus—the man who became the Apostle
Paul. The Old Testament was important to him. He had the following
to say about what had been written beforehand.

> These things happened to them as a warning to us. All this
> was written in the Scriptures to teach us who live in these last
> days (1 Corinthians 10:11 CEV).

Paul said that what was written in the Scripture was to teach us how to
live. It is a divinely inspired document.

There is something else. Even while the New Testament was being written and cited as authoritative Scripture, the Old Testament was still
used and cited alongside it. Both testaments were considered divinely
authoritative by the early Christians.

MANY CENTRAL TRUTHS ABOUT GOD ARE REVEALED IN THE OLD TESTAMENT

Without the Old Testament, the New Testament makes no sense whatsoever. Many of the major teachings of the Bible are given to us in the Old Testament. For example, from the Old Testament we learn such central truths as God exists and that He created the universe and everything in it. We also learn that human beings were originally created perfect but fell from that position because of sin.

In addition, we discover that forgiveness of sin based upon sacrifice. These are just a few of the many central truths that we learn from the Old Testament.

1. THE OLD TESTAMENT PREDICTS THE COMING OF THE MESSIAH, OR THE CHRIST INTO THE WORLD

The Old Testament gives us the predictions of a Savior, the Messiah or the Christ, who will come into the world. He will be the One who will save people from their sins. Without the Old Testament, we would not know that the Messiah is coming or why He needs to come into the world. Furthermore, we would not know how to identify Him when He does arrive.

2. IT GIVES THE HISTORY OF GOD'S CHOSEN PEOPLE-ISRAEL

The Old Testament gives us the major events in the history of God's chosen people—the Jews. It records their origin, history, their exile, and their return. The Scripture shows their place in the overall plan of God and in His unfolding plan of redemption for the human race. It shows the nation prospered when they obeyed God.

3. IT PRESENTS SOME DETAILS OF THE FUTURE RULE OF CHRIST THAT ARE NOT FOUND IN THE NEW TESTAMENT

The Bible, in both testaments, speaks of the kingdom of God coming to the earth. There are details in the Old Testament about this coming

93

kingdom that are not found in the New Testament. Without the Old Testament, we would not know many of these details.

IT HAS AN ENORMOUS AMOUNT OF MATERIAL THAT IS HELPFUL FOR SPIRITUAL GROWTH

The Old Testament contains much devotional material that is still practical for the believer. Even today, Christians can learn valuable spiritual truths from studying its pages. These truths are everlasting.

The list goes on and on. Therefore, far from being outdated or irrelevant, the Old Testament has tremendous value for the believer today.

SUMMARY TO QUESTION 5
WHAT VALUE DOES THE OLD TESTAMENT HAVE?

Though it is often neglected in favor of the New Testament, the Old Testament is absolutely necessary for the believer to study. The Old Testament is the foundation for the New Testament. It prepared the world for the coming of Christ. In fact, without it the New Testament makes no sense whatever.

Many reasons can be given for the importance of the Old Testament. For one thing, it was the only sacred Scripture of Jesus, His disciples, and the first century Jews. The Old Testament was continually cited as authoritative while the New Testament was being written—it still had value for them.

In fact, many of the basic truths about God come from the Old Testament. Without the Old Testament, we would not know the predictions and promises God made of the coming Deliverer or Messiah. The Old Testament also chronicles the history of God's chosen people— Israel. The Old Testament also provides details of the future reign of Jesus Christ upon the earth—details not contained in the New Testament. In short, the Old Testament is essential for study.

QUESTION 6

What Value Does
the New Testament Have?

The Old Testament has much value for believers today. However, the Old Testament is incomplete. God gave humanity a "new" testament or covenant. There is immense value in studying this New Testament. We will highlight a few of the many reasons. They are as follows.

1. THE NEW TESTAMENT RECORDS THE FULFILLMENT OF THE OLD TESTAMENT PREDICTIONS ABOUT THE MESSIAH

The Old Testament gives the predictions, or promises, of the coming Messiah, while the New Testament records their fulfillment. The Old Testament writers looked forward to the day when the Christ would appear, while the New Testament records the testimony of those who saw and heard Him. Without the New Testament, we would assume humanity is still waiting for God to fulfill these promises.

2. IT EXPLAINS HOW GOD BECAME A HUMAN BEING

The New Testament informs us that God became a human being in the Person of Jesus Christ. The key verse of the New Testament reads as follows.

> And the Word became flesh and dwelt among us, and we have seen his glory, glory as of the only Son from the Father, full of grace and truth (John 1:14 ESV).

The living God became a human being, and lived among humanity, in the Person of Jesus Christ. We only know about this from the New Testament. Nowhere else.

3. IT GIVES THE PLAN OF SALVATION TO LOST SINNERS

The reason for the coming of Christ to earth was to provide salvation for lost sinners. Jesus made clear His purpose. He said.

> For the Son of Man has come to seek and to save the lost (Luke 19:10 HCSB).

He is the only way in which a person can have a relationship with the one God. We read the following in John's gospel.

> Jesus said to him, "I am the way, the truth, and the life. No one comes to the Father except through Me" (John 14:6 NKJV).

This is only revealed in the New Testament.

4. IT TELLS US WHAT WILL HAPPEN IN THIS PRESENT AGE

We are now in an interval between the two comings of Christ. Jesus Christ is currently building His church on the earth. The church is not a physical building but rather a group of people who have believed in Him. Nothing will stop the building of the church. Jesus made this promise.

> Now I say to you that you are Peter, and upon this rock I will build my church, and all the powers of hell will not conquer it (Matthew 16:18 NLT).

Gods' work will continue through His people, the church, until Christ comes back.

5. IT INFORMS US WHAT WILL HAPPEN IN THE FUTURE

The New Testament also tells us about God's coming kingdom. It adds details that are not found in the Old Testament. It supplements our knowledge about how God will bring His everlasting kingdom through the Second Coming of Jesus Christ to the earth. The Bible says.

> Look! He is coming with the clouds; every eye will see him, even those who pierced him; and on his account all the tribes of the earth will wail. So it is to be. Amen (Revelation 1:7 NRSV).

We now know what the future holds because of the teaching of the New Testament.

6. IT TELLS US HOW TO LIVE THE CHRISTIAN LIFE

Once a person believes in Jesus Christ, there are instructions given as to what they should do next. These are found exclusively in the New Testament. For example, Paul wrote to the Galatians.

> Carry one another's burdens; in this way you will fulfill the law of Christ (Galatians 6:2 HCSB).

Commandments like these inform believers in Jesus Christ how they are to behave. We know how we are to conduct our lives because it is revealed to us in the New Testament.

Therefore, along with the Old Testament, the New Testament should be our source of serious study about God and His plans for the world. There are many reasons as to why this is so.

SUMMARY TO QUESTION 6
WHAT VALUE DOES THE NEW TESTAMENT HAVE?

As was true with the Old Testament, the New Testament is an absolutely essential document for study. In it we find the fulfillment of the promises that were recorded in the Old Testament. We discover that God did indeed send the Messiah—Jesus of Nazareth. In addition, we find that Jesus was more than a mere human being; He was actually the eternal God who became human on our behalf. The purpose of His coming is also outlined in the New Testament.

We know that He came to die for the sins of the world. Once a person trusts what Jesus did on their behalf, they go about living the Christian life. The New Testament instructs them concerning how they should live it. The New Testament also lets us know what will happen in the future. We know that Jesus Christ will come to the earth a second time and set up His eternal kingdom. All these truths, along with many more, are found only in the New Testament.

Therefore, it is necessary that both testaments of Scripture be given serious study by those who want to know God's truth.

Why Are the Books of the Bible
Placed in A Particular Order or Sequence?

Although Christians believe that the sixty-six books of the Bible are all part of sacred Scripture, the books are not arranged in any God-given order. The reasons for the way they are variously arranged are as follows.

THE OLD TESTAMENT (PROTESTANT ORDER)

According to the Protestant order, the books of the Old Testament are divided along a topical arrangement. They are divided into five sections. This is for the sake of convenience. The usual Protestant order is as follows: The Law, History, Poetry, Major Prophets, Minor Prophets.

This division goes back to the time the Old Testament was translated from Hebrew into Greek. This translation, known as the Septuagint (which means seventy and is abbreviated LXX), began in the third century before Christ. Jerome, the scholar who translated the Old Testament into Latin in the fourth century A.D., also adapted this division. The present English division follows Jerome.

THE HEBREW DIVISION OF SCRIPTURE

The traditional number of the books contained in the Hebrew Scripture is twenty-four. First century writer Flavius Josephus said the Jews recognized twenty-two sacred books. Most likely he placed Ruth with

Judges and Lamentations with Jeremiah. Both the Protestant division and the Hebrew division contain the exact same books, no more, no less. The only difference is in the way in which these books are divided.

An apocryphal book, called Second Esdras, which was written at the end of the first century A.D., records what is known as the "Ezra legend." In it, we find the number of books listed as twenty-four.

There was also another ancient Hebrew division where the books were numbered at twenty-seven. Again, the contents were exactly the same as those divisions that had twenty-two and twenty-four books. They were merely divided differently.

Modern Hebrew Bibles have thirty-six books. The books of Samuel, Kings, and Chronicles are considered one book, not two. The Protestant Bible divides Samuel, Kings, and Chronicles into two books following the Septuagint.

The reason that the Septuagint divided these three books into six books was for practical reasons—they could not all fit onto one scroll. The Hebrew text does not contain vowels, and thus it is much shorter than the Greek text. Therefore, the entire book could be put onto one scroll.

However, the Greek language contains vowels and thus two scrolls were needed to record the entire book. Hence, we end up with First and Second Samuel, First and Second Kings, and First and Second Chronicles. Again, we have the exact same text—the only difference is the way it is divided.

There is something else that should be noted. The terms Major Prophets and Minor Prophets are derived from the size of the writings—it has nothing to do with their importance. The Major Prophets are longer writings than the Minor Prophets.

SOME GROUPS ACCEPT MORE OLD TESTAMENT BOOKS THAN PROTESTANTS AND JEWS

The Roman Catholic Church, the Orthodox Church, and the Ethiopic Church, add a number of books to the Old Testament that are not accepted by the Protestants, or by the Jews. As far as the books added by the Roman Catholic Church is concerned, these works are known as the "Old Testament Apocrypha" by Protestants and Jews, and "Deuterocanonical books," or books added to the canon, by the Roman Catholic Church.

In our book on the "Are Some Books Missing From The Bible," we detail the reasons as to why the Roman Catholic Church accepts these works as Scripture and why Protestantism and Judaism reject them. We will discover that there are no good reasons for accepting these extra books as part of Holy Scripture.

The Orthodox Church adds three or four additional books that the Roman Catholic Church does not consider to be sacred Scripture, while the Ethiopic Church adds five books.

THE HEBREW BIBLE TODAY HAS THREE MAJOR DIVISIONS

The modern Hebrew Bible has a different structure than the English Bible. The grouping of books is according to their literary character. The Hebrew Bible divides the Scripture into three divisions—the Law, the Prophets, and the Writings. The Hebrew terms are *Torah, Nebhiim,* and *Kethubiim.* The acronym TeNaKh is used to describe the entire collection (*Torah, Nebhiim,* and *Kethubiim*).

One note of interest is that certain books of history, Joshua through Kings, are called books of prophecy. The reason this is so is because history and prophecy are closely intermingled in these written works. There is the historical event recorded and then the divine explanation, or meaning, given for the event.

THERE MAY BE EARLY TESTIMONY TO THE THREEFOLD DIVISION OF THE OLD TESTAMENT

There is some question as to whether that at the time of Christ, there was the threefold division of the Old Testament, the Law, the Prophets, and the Writings, with the exact same books in each section. The first clear testimony to this threefold division, with the same contents in each section of the Old Testament, is about a century *after* Christ.

Some have argued that earliest testimony to the threefold division of the Old Testament, with the same books in each section, actually goes back two hundred years before the time of Christ. It is found in the prologue to apocryphal book of Ecclesiasticus—written about 180 B.C. However, it is not certain that this work testifies to this same threefold division with the same books in each of these three sections.

First century historian, Flavius Josephus, has a threefold division of the Old Testament but it does not contain the same books in each section as does the modern division of Scripture.

Jesus referred to a threefold division of the Old Testament. We read about this in Luke's gospel.

> He [Jesus] said to them, "This is what I told you while I was still with you: Everything must be fulfilled that is written about me in the Law of Moses, the Prophets and the Psalms" (Luke 24:44 NIV).

He called the last part "the Psalms." It is possible that only the Book of Psalms, by itself, constituted a third division of the Old Testament. All of the other books were either in the Law or the Prophets.

Philo of Alexandria, who lived in the first century A.D., mentioned the three different sections of the Old Testament (*The Contemplative Life* 25). Like Jesus, he calls the third section "the Psalms." Again, we may have only the Book of Psalms in this third division—and not all the books that eventually made up the third division of the Hebrew canon. The evidence is not that clear and scholars are divided on how to understand it.

THE USUAL DIVISION WAS INTO TWO SECTIONS: LAW AND PROPHETS

The Old Testament was usually divided into two sections—the Law and the Prophets. This division consisted of the Books of Moses, the Law, and all the books that came after Moses. Jesus referred to this division. In the Sermon on the Mount, we read the following.

> So in everything, do to others what you would have them do to you, for this sums up the Law and the Prophets (Matthew 7:12 NIV).

The New Testament uses both the twofold division, as well as the threefold division, in referring to the Old Testament books. However, as stated, it is uncertain that the modern threefold division was used during New Testament times with the same books in each of the three sections.

THE OLD TESTAMENT BOOKS ARE DIVIDED DIFFERENTLY BY JEWS AND CHRISTIANS

It is clear that the order of the Old Testament books has not always been the same. In addition, both the Jews and the Christians have divided the books differently. We can sum up the various divisions of the Old Testament as follows.

ANCIENT HEBREW DIVISION ACCORDING TO JOSEPHUS (22 BOOKS)

The ancient Hebrew division has twenty-two books. The Book of Ruth was probably placed with Judges while Lamentations was placed with Jeremiah. This division is testified to by Josephus as well as by the early church father Origen. It is possible that the division into twenty-two books was to symbolize the twenty-two letters of the Hebrew alphabet.

ANCIENT HEBREW DIVISION ACCORDING TO SECOND ESDRAS, THE EZRA LEGEND (24 BOOKS)

Another ancient Hebrew division, found in a work called Second Esdras, lists the number of books at twenty-four. Again, we have the same content—just a different way of dividing them.

ANCIENT HEBREW DIVISION ACCORDING TO JEROME (27 BOOKS)

The fourth century Bible translator, Jerome, mentions another ancient Hebrew division where the books are numbered at twenty-seven.

MODERN HEBREW DIVISION (36 BOOKS)

Modern Hebrew division is thirty-six books. The Twelve Minor Prophets are not considered as one book but as separate books in the modern division.

PROTESTANT DIVISION (39 BOOKS)

The Protestant division has thirty-nine books. They contain the exact same content as the ancient and modern Hebrew divisions—the differences are in the way the books are counted.

Though the divisions are different, these books contain the exact same content. Therefore, the Jews and Protestants agree on the extent of the Old Testament canon.

MORE BOOKS ARE ADDED BY THE ROMAN CATHOLICS, THE ORTHODOX CHURCH AND THE ETHIOPIC CHURCH

The Roman Catholic Church, the Orthodox Church, as well as the Ethiopic Church, add more books to the Old Testament than do the Jews and Protestants. These can be listed as follows.

ROMAN CATHOLIC DIVISION (46 BOOKS)

The Roman Catholic division has forty-six books in the Old Testament. This is because the Old Testament Apocrypha, consisting of seven books, is added to the thirty-nine books of the Hebrew Scripture. With the addition of these books, the total comes to forty-six separate books.

EASTERN, GREEK ORTHODOX DIVISION (49 BOOKS)

The Eastern Orthodox Church, like the Roman Catholic Church, adds the seven books from the Apocrypha to the Old Testament. They also seemingly add three other books that the Roman Catholic Church does not. The reason we say "seemingly" is because they are somewhat vague on the exact status of these extra books.

RUSSIAN ORTHODOX DIVISION (50 BOOKS)

The Russian Orthodox Church adds the same books to the Old Testament as the Roman Catholic Church. In addition, four other books, that Roman Catholics do not accept as canonical, are also seemingly added to their Old Testament. Like the Greek Orthodox Church, the Russian Orthodox Church is also vague on the exact number of books which make up the Old Testament.

THE ETHIOPIC CHURCH DIVISION (51 BOOKS)

The Ethiopic Church accepts the same forty-nine books as does the Eastern, or Greek Orthodox Church, as well as adding two others—the Book of Jubilees and the Book of Enoch. They are the only major Christian community that accepts these two books as part of Old Testament Scripture.

THE THIRTY-NINE BOOKS OF THE OLD TESTAMENT ARE NOT IN DISPUTE

To sum up, there is no dispute among the Christians with respect to the thirty-nine books which are presently contained in the Old Testament. All agree that these books belong in Holy Scripture. The question is this: are there additional books that should also be considered divinely inspired and be added to the Old Testament?

THE DIVISION OF NEW TESTAMENT SCRIPTURE

As far as the New Testament is concerned, Protestantism, Roman Catholicism, and the Orthodox Church accepts the same thirty-nine books as divinely inspired Scripture—there are no differences between them.

OBSERVATIONS ON THE PRESENT DIVISION OF SCRIPTURE

There are a number of things that should be noted about the present division of Scripture that is found in printed Bibles. They include the following.

1. THERE IS NO DIVINE ORDER TO THE BOOKS OF THE OLD TESTAMENT

To begin with, there is no divine or sacred order in which the books of the Old Testament are to be placed. It is only in modern times that the books have been placed in a consistent order. The reason has to do with the invention of printing. Once the Old Testament began to be printed, the order of the books became somewhat standardized.

The order of the books for the Old Testament in the English Bible is derived from the Latin Vulgate. It was the standard translation for western Christianity for a thousand years. In the Old Testament, the Greek translation of the Hebrew Old Testament, the Septuagint, is usually seen as the basis of the order of the books which are found in the Vulgate. Yet the manuscripts of the Septuagint have much variation in them.

The Hebrew and Greek manuscripts of the Old Testament usually have the same order for the five books of Moses and for the four books of the prophets, or history, Joshua, Judges, Samuel, and Kings, which come after the Books of Moses. Yet this is not always the case. For example, the Syriac Peshitta, an ancient translation of the Old Testament, has the Book of Job between the Books of Moses and the Book of Joshua. This occurred because it was believed that Moses wrote the Book of Job.

We also find that there was no settled order in the remaining books of the Hebrew Scriptures. The Hebrew order is different from the Greek order. The Hebrew order consists of the Law, Prophets and Writings while the Greek order has the Law, History, Poetry, and Prophets. English versions have followed the Greek order of the books, through the Latin, rather than the Hebrew order.

Consequently, today we find the printed Hebrew texts of the Old Testament having a different order than the books which are found in the English versions. The contents are the same but the order of the books is different. Therefore, there is no proper or divine order in which we are to read or study the Old Testament books.

2. THERE IS NO SACRED ORDER OR SEQUENCE FOR THE BOOKS OF THE NEW TESTAMENT

The same problem arises with the New Testament books. The twenty-seven books are not placed in the order in which they were written. The order is more logical than chronological. However, this order is not always consistently found in the ancient manuscripts. Indeed, in the existing Latin manuscripts that contain parts of the New Testament we find almost three hundred different sequences for the books!

The first known listing of our present twenty-seven New Testament books is contained in an Easter letter written and sent out by the church Father Athanasius in A.D. 367. In his list, the general or universal letters follow the Book of Acts, and the Book of Hebrews follows Second Thessalonians. The first list of the New Testament books in the order most people are familiar with, is found in the writings of Amphilocius of Iconium in A.D. 380.

When the books were written on individual scrolls their sequence did not matter. The various scrolls were kept in a chest or box called a capsa. However, once the codex, or book form, was invented in the second century A.D., the order or sequence became more of an issue.

3. THE ORDER OF THE GOSPELS IS BASED UPON THE ASSUMED ORDER IN WHICH THEY WERE WRITTEN

The common or traditional order of the four gospels, Matthew, Mark, Luke, and John is based upon the way the four gospels are found in the great majority of manuscripts of the New Testament. Matthew is usually the first, followed by Mark, then Luke, and John the last.

For most of the history of the church, this was the order in which people believed they were written. However, many modern scholars now assume that Mark was written first. But this is by no means certain. To the contrary, every ancient source testifies that Matthew was the first gospel written. Whatever the case may be, there is no "divine" order to the four gospels.

Indeed, there are at least eight other sequences in which we find the four gospels in the various manuscripts of the New Testament. For example, in some manuscripts written in the fifth century, the order is Matthew, John, Mark and Luke. Since Matthew and John were the only two apostles among the four gospel writers, it is easy to understand why some would place them before the other written gospels. Interestingly, Luke's gospel is *never* placed first in any of the manuscripts and Matthew's gospel is *never* placed last.

4. THE BOOK OF ACTS IS USUALLY PLACED AFTER THE FOUR GOSPELS

Since the Book of Acts is the transitional book from the gospels to the New Testament letters, it was usually placed after the four gospels. However, this is not always the case. *Codex Sinaiticus*, the oldest complete Greek manuscript of the New Testament, as well as a sixth century manuscript, *Codex Fuldensis*, places the Book of Acts after the letters of Paul. Interestingly, this sequence is found in the first printed Greek New Testament—volume five of the Complutensian Polyglot printed in 1514. This again underscores the fact that there is no divine sequence, or order, of the New Testament books.

5. THE LETTERS OF PAUL ARE NOT ALWAYS PLACED BEFORE THE UNIVERSAL LETTERS

There is still more. In the present printed editions of the New Testament in the Western Church, the letters of Paul are placed before the general or universal letters. In the Eastern Church, this is reversed—the general or universal letters come before Paul's writings in the printed editions. Indeed, almost all the Greek manuscripts of the New Testament have the universal letters directly *after* the Book of Acts and before the letters of Paul.

This is likely due to the fact that the universal letters were addressed to all believers while Paul's letters were written to specific churches as well as to private individuals.

In addition, three of the authors of the Catholic letters, James, Peter, and John, were considered "pillars" of the church. On the other hand, according to his own testimony, Paul was the least of the apostles. This could be part of the reason why his letters came after the universal letters.

6. THE PRESENT ORDER OF PAUL'S WRITINGS IS SEEMINGLY BASED UPON THEIR SIZE

The present order of the thirteen letters of the Apostle Paul is not based upon when they were written, but rather it is seemingly based according to their length. The Book of Romans is the longest letter that Paul wrote to the churches, while Second Thessalonians is the shortest. The only exception to this is Ephesians—which is slightly longer than Galatians. First Timothy is the longest letter that Paul wrote to an individual, while Philemon is the shortest.

However, this usual order of Paul's writings is not consistently found in biblical manuscripts. There are about twenty different arrangements of Paul's letters that have been found in biblical manuscripts.

7. THE UNIVERSAL LETTERS ARE NOT ALWAYS IN THE SAME SEQUENCE

Like the other groupings of the New Testament, the order in which we find the general, or universal, letters is not always same in the existing manuscripts. They were commonly found in the sequence of James, Peter, John, and Jude. This sequence is the same in which we find these names listed in the Book of Galatians. Paul wrote.

> And when James, Cephas, and John, who seemed to be pillars, perceived the grace that had been given to me, they gave me and Barnabas the right hand of fellowship, that we should go to the Gentiles and they to the circumcised (Galatians 2:9 NKJV).

We should note that "Cephas" is the Aramaic name for Peter.

Thus, the listing of these three universal letters in this particular sequence may have been influenced by the order in which Paul listed these men.

In the Western church, the supremacy of Peter eventually came to be an important doctrine. Thus, we find Peter's writings listed *first* among the universal letters.

8. THE BOOK OF HEBREWS IS FOUND IN NUMEROUS PLACES

While the Book of Hebrews is classified as one of the universal letters, it is found in a number of different places in the manuscripts of the New Testament—often with the letters of Paul. In most of the Greek manuscripts, we find Hebrews following Philemon. In the oldest surviving manuscript copy that contains the Book of Hebrews, P46, it is found after the Book of Romans. In a number of ancient manuscripts Hebrews stands between the Second Thessalonians and First Timothy.

Part of the reason can be attributed to the confusion over who authored Hebrews. Many attributed it to Paul and thus placed it somewhere among Paul's letters. It has been speculated that at an early time,

Hebrews was kept in a box, or *capsa*, with Paul's letters. Therefore, it was assumed that Paul was the actual author. Whatever the case may be, Hebrews has an unsettled history in its placement among the New Testament books.

9. THE BOOK OF REVELATION WAS USUALLY PLACED LAST AMONG THE BOOKS LISTED

The Book of Revelation, or the Apocalypse, was usually placed as the final book in the New Testament manuscripts. However, this was not always the case. In a few manuscripts, it is placed after the four gospels. This occurred because it contains the words of Christ which were written to the seven churches. Consequently, it seemed appropriate to put a book with the actual words of Christ after the four gospels.

Therefore, as we consider the position of the books of the New Testament, we find that the five main groupings, Gospels, Acts, Letters of Paul, Universal or Catholic Letters, and Revelation, are not always in the same order. In addition, the various books that are found in each of these groupings are likewise not always in the same sequence. Evidently, it was not a great concern to the believers as to the order or sequence in which they placed or read the various books of the New Testament.

10. GENESIS AND REVELATION ARE IN THE RIGHT POSITION IN THE PRINTED TEXTS

From the above evidence, we can conclude that the books of the Bible, as found in printed English editions, are not in any sacred order but rather are usually found in a logical order. However, two of them, Genesis and Revelation, should stand in their present position. The Book of Genesis must be the first book of Scripture because it records the beginning of all created things. In the same manner, the Book of Revelation should stand last because it chronicles the end of all things that presently exist—as well as the promise of a new heaven and a new earth.

11. THE TITLES OF THE BOOKS ARE BASED UPON THEIR MAIN CHARACTER, CONTENTS, LITERARY FORM, OR PEOPLE ADDRESSED

Not only is there no such thing as a sacred order or sequence for the books of Scripture, there is also no such thing as a sacred or a divine name or title for these books. Originally, the books did not have a title written at the beginning of the work. However, there was probably some notation made on the outside of the scroll to indicate either who wrote it or what the writing was about.

For the most part, the English titles of the various Old Testament books are derived from the Latin Vulgate. These titles were translated from the Septuagint, the Greek translation of the Hebrew Old Testament.

However, the titles of the first five books of the Hebrew Scripture, or the Books of Moses, differ from the English titles. The Hebrew titles are based upon the first few words in the text. For example in Hebrew, Genesis is called "In the beginning," Exodus is titled, "These are the names," Leviticus, "And he called," Numbers is "In the wilderness" and Deuteronomy, "These are the words." The English titles of these first books come to us through the Latin Vulgate by way of the Septuagint.

Other Old Testament books are based upon the names of the main character, such as Ruth or Esther, the contents of the book, Judges, Kings, Chronicles, or the author of the book such as Isaiah, Ezekiel, or Jeremiah. The Psalms and Proverbs are named after their literary form— they contain songs and wise sayings.

In the New Testament, we find that the four gospels were named after the individuals whom it is believed authored the works—Matthew, Mark, Luke and John. Properly, we should speak of the gospel "according to Matthew," "according to Mark," etc., rather than the gospel "of Matthew." The gospel is the good news about Jesus—according to the various authors.

Interestingly, the Book of Acts, or the Acts of the Apostles, did not initially have this for a title until the end of the second century. In some manuscripts, the Book of Acts is wrongly titled "the Acts of All the Apostles." The Book of Acts does not record the acts of all the apostles but rather only a select few.

Paul's letters are named after either the churches to whom he was writing (such as Thessalonica) or the individuals to whom he addressed (such as Timothy).

In contrast to Paul's letters, the universal letters are named after the person who it is believed authored the letters—Peter, James, Jude, and John—rather than the recipients of the letters as is the case with the letters of Paul.

The Book of Revelation is somewhat unique. The manuscripts that contain the Book of Revelation have a number of different titles. They include "The Revelation of John;" "The Revelation of John the Evangelist;" and "The Revelation of John the Divine." However, the first verse tells us that this writing is "the revelation of Jesus Christ"—not the revelation of John. John merely wrote down what the Lord showed him.

From the above facts, we should view the titles of the various books of Scripture as a means of helping us understand the contents of the writing but not as some sacred or divine heading.

ALMOST ALL OF THE BOOKS OF THE BIBLE WERE WRITTEN BY JEWS

It appears that men from the Hebrew, or Jewish race, wrote all the books of the Scripture. Scripture says that the Jews were entrusted with the very words of God. We read the following.

> What advantage, then, is there in being a Jew, or what value is there in circumcision? Much in every way! First of all, the Jews have been entrusted with the very words of God (Romans 3:1,2 NIV).

The one exception are the writings of Luke. He wrote the gospel that bears his name, as well as the Book of Acts. It seems that Luke was a Gentile. Paul spoke of him in this manner.

> Luke, the dearly loved physician, and Demas greet you (Colossians 4:14 HCSB).

Before he sent greetings from Luke, Paul made this statement.

> So does Jesus who is called Justus. These alone of the circumcision are my coworkers for the kingdom of God, and they have been a comfort to me (Colossians 4:11 HCSB).

After Paul mentioned the various Jews who provided comfort to him, he then went on to mention a number of Gentiles. Luke is in this group of people. Therefore, it seems Luke is associated with the Gentiles, or non-Jews, who sent their greetings.

CONCLUSION: THE SEQUENCE DOES NOT MATTER

In conclusion, these facts, concerning the present order of the biblical books, help us understand the total number of books that are considered as Scripture, as well as the order in which we presently find them. The real issue is not so much the order or sequence of the books, the real question is this: do we have the correct books in the Old Testament and in the New Testament? The answer to this question is a resounding, "Yes!"

SUMMARY TO QUESTION 7
WHY ARE THE BOOKS OF THE BIBLE PLACED IN A PARTICULAR ORDER?

The books of the Bible are divided for sake of convenience and their logical historical development—there is no sacred order. Because the order of the books is human-made, it is not necessary to read the Bible in this sequence.

In the Protestant Bible there are sixty-six books—thirty-nine in the Old Testament and twenty-seven in the New Testament. In the Hebrew Bible, which has the same content as the Protestant Old Testament, there are twenty-four books. The difference is in the way they are divided.

The Roman Catholic Church, Eastern Orthodox Church, Russian Orthodox, and Ethiopic Church, add a number of books to the Old Testament that are not accepted by Protestants, or by the Jews. These books are known as the Apocrypha by Protestants, and the deuterocanonical books by the Roman Catholic Church.

There are twenty-seven books in the New Testament. They can be divided into four gospels, one book of history, twenty-one letters, and one book of prophecy.

There is no divine order for the biblical books. In the Latin manuscripts that are known to exist, we find about three hundred different arrangements of the books of Scripture. Paul's letters are arranged in at least twenty different sequences.

The four gospels are placed in their present order based on the usual order in which they are found in the existing manuscripts. The letters of Paul are placed in order according to their length rather than the time they were written.

The Eastern and Western Churches have a different order with respect to Paul's writings and the general letters. The Western Church places Paul's writings before the general letters, while the Eastern churches reverse this.

While there is no sacred order of the books of Scripture, Genesis and Revelation must stand first and last since they detail the beginning and the end of all things.

The books of the Bible were named after their subject matter, literary style, person or group addressed, or the name of the author. All the books seem to have been written by Jews with the exception of the writings of Luke (Luke/Acts).

These are the basic facts concerning the order and number of the books that presently make up the Bible.

Why Is the Bible Divided Into Chapters and Verses?

Today, when we want to find a passage of Scripture, we look it up under its chapter and verse. Where did these divisions come from? Are they found in the original writings? If not, who decided how the sacred writings should be divided?

THERE WERE NO CHAPTER OR VERSE DIVISIONS IN THE ORIGINAL

When the books of the Bible were originally written there were no such things as chapters or verses. Each book was written without any breaks from the beginning to the end. Consequently, there are a number of important observations that need to be made about the present chapter and verse divisions that we find in Scripture.

OBSERVATION 1: THE BOOKS HAVE BEEN DIVIDED INTO CHAPTERS AND VERSES FOR CONVENIENCE

The chapter and verse divisions were added to the Bible for the sake of convenience. There is no authoritative basis for the divisions we now find. For the greater part of human history, there have been no chapter or verse divisions in Scripture.

OBSERVATION 2: THE ORIGIN OF CHAPTER DIVISIONS

The divisions of individual books of Scripture into smaller sections began as early as the fourth century A.D. Codex Vaticanus, a fourth century Greek manuscript, used paragraph divisions. These were comparable to what we find in manuscripts of the Hebrew Bible.

In the fifth century, the biblical translator Jerome divided Scripture into short potions, or passages, called pericopes. The word is still used today to refer to a self-contained unit of Scripture. His work proceeded the dividing of Scripture into chapters.

The actual chapter division took place much later. A man named Stephen Langton divided the Bible into chapters in the year A.D. 1227. The Bible he used was the Latin Vulgate. Langton was a professor at the University of Paris at the time. Later, he became the Archbishop of Canterbury.

These chapter divisions were later transferred to the Hebrew text in the fourteenth century by a man named Salomon ben Ishmael. There seems to have been certain changes made by Salomon ben Ishmael because the chapter divisions in the Hebrew text do not line up exactly with the English Bible.

OBSERVATION 3: THE ORIGIN OF VERSE DIVISIONS

The modern Old Testament division into verses was standardized by the Ben Asher family around A.D. 900. However, the practice of dividing the Old Testament books into verses goes back centuries earlier.

Modern verse division for the New Testament was the work of Robert Stephanus (Stephens), a French printer. He divided the Greek text into verses for his Greek New Testament published in 1551.

The first entire Bible, in which these chapter and verse divisions were used, was Stephen's edition of the Latin Vulgate (1555).

The first English Bible to have both chapter and verse divisions was the Geneva Bible (1560).

OBSERVATION 4: CHAPTERS AND VERSES ARE HELPFUL FOR REFERENCE AND QUOTATION

The chapter and verse divisions are convenient for reference and quotation purposes. They make it easier to find certain statements and accounts in Scripture.

It must always be remembered that the divisions into chapters and verses are human-made. They are sometimes arbitrary, and they sometimes interfere with the sense of the passage. The first step in Bible interpretation is to ignore the modern chapter and verse divisions.

OBSERVATION 5: THE CHAPTER DIVISIONS CAN CAUSE PROBLEMS

Indeed, the divisions into chapters and verses can actually cause some problems. There are instances where chapters are wrongly divided. For example, the end of Matthew chapter 16 should actually be placed with the beginning of Matthew 17.

Matthew 16 ends with Jesus saying the following.

> And I assure you that some of you standing here right now will not die before you see me, the Son of Man, coming in my Kingdom (Matthew 16:28 NLT).

The next verse reads.

> Six days later, Jesus took with him Peter and James and his brother John and led them up a high mountain, by themselves (Matthew 17:1 NRSV).

This verse should have been in the same chapter as the previous verse since it is continuing the story. This unfortunate chapter division is not an isolated example. Indeed, there are a number of illustrations which we could cite.

OBSERVATION 6: THE VERSE DIVISIONS CAN ALSO CAUSE PROBLEMS

Dividing the Bible into verses can also give the impression that the Scripture consists of a number or maxims or wise sayings. For example, Paul wrote to the Colossians.

> Don't handle, don't eat, don't touch! (Colossians 2:21 NLT).

This verse, by itself, gives the impression that Scripture encourages some type of physical self-denial. Yet just the opposite is true. In context, Paul is actually teaching against this type of behavior. His argument is as follows.

> You have died with Christ, and he has set you free from the evil powers of this world. So why do you keep on following rules of the world, such as Don't handle, don't eat, don't touch! (Colossians 2:20,21 NLT).

The next verse emphasizes that such restrictions are human commandments—not commandments from God.

> Such rules are mere human teaching about things that are gone as soon as we use them (Colossians 2:22 NLT).

When we read the verse in context it says the following.

> You have died with Christ, and he has set you free from the evil powers of this world. So why do you keep on following rules of the world, such as, "Don't handle, don't eat, don't touch." Such rules are mere human teaching about things that are gone as soon as we use them. These rules may seem wise because they require strong devotion, humility, and severe bodily discipline. But they have no effect when it comes to conquering a person's evil thoughts and desires (Colossians 2:20-23 NLT).

Therefore, this one verse, when read on its own, gives the wrong impression of the biblical teaching. This is one of the problems with the Bible divided into verses—people will isolate the verses from the rest of the context.

Many more examples could be listed. Indeed, one could argue that the Bible teaches atheism.

> There is no God (Psalm 14:1 NIV).

Of course, the complete verse reads as follows.

> The fool says in his heart, "There is no God." They are corrupt, their deeds are vile; there is no one who does good (Psalm 14:1 NIV)

Others could contend that Jesus taught cannibalism! The Gospel of John records Jesus saying the following.

> So Jesus said to them, "I assure you: Unless you eat the flesh of the Son of Man and drink His blood, you do not have life in yourselves. Anyone who eats My flesh and drinks My blood has eternal life, and I will raise him up on the last day, because My flesh is true food and My blood is true drink. The one who eats My flesh and drinks My blood lives in Me, and I in him" (John 6: 53-56 HCSB).

This is why it is important to read each particular verse in context. Otherwise, one can make the Bible say things that it does not want to say.

OBSERVATION 7: CHAPTERS AND VERSES ARE NOT WHAT THE AUTHORS INTENDED

In sum, the original authors of Scripture did not intend that their writings be divided up into chapters or verses. They intended that the books be read straight through from the beginning. A number of the books of Scripture can be read through in one sitting. This is the best way to discover what the author is trying to say.

In addition, dividing up the Scripture into chapters and verses encourages people to read only small parts at a time. This is not always helpful. This is why the Bible should be read the same way as the original authors intended it to be read.

SUMMARY TO QUESTION 8
WHY IS THE BIBLE DIVIDED INTO CHAPTERS AND VERSES?

In the original text of the various books of the Bible there are no such things as chapter and verse divisions. They were added later for the sake of convenience. While they are helpful, they are not authoritative in any sense of the term. In fact, they can cause a number of problems.

Chapter and verse divisions give the impression that the Scripture should be read and studied in bits and pieces. This is not what the original authors intended. The entire context must always be considered. Consequently, the chapter and verse divisions should be ignored when one attempts to properly interpret the entire message of Scripture.

What Symbols, or Word Pictures, Does the Bible Use to Describe Itself?

The Bible uses a variety of symbols or word pictures to describe itself. They give us a better understanding of the character of the Word of God. The word pictures found in Scripture include the following symbols.

1. MILK

Milk is used as an example of what new believers partake. Peter wrote.

> Like newborn babies, crave pure spiritual milk, so that by it you may grow up in your salvation, now that you have tasted that the Lord is good (1 Peter 2:2-3 NIV).

However, as believers mature in their faith they need to go beyond the "milk stage." The writer to the Hebrews compared milk to solid food. He wrote.

> For though by this time you ought to be teachers, you need someone to teach you again the basic principles of God's revelation. You need milk, not solid food. Now everyone who lives on milk is inexperienced with the message about righteousness, because he is an infant. But solid food is for the mature—for those whose senses have been trained to distinguish between good and evil (Hebrews 5:12-14 HCSB).

The people to whom this letter was addressed should have advanced beyond the "milk" stage. Yet, they had not.

2. SOLID FOOD

As we just observed, Scripture is also symbolized by solid food. This speaks of maturity, while milk speaks of infancy. Paul wrote the following to the Corinthians.

> Dear brothers and sisters, when I was with you I couldn't talk to you as I would to mature Christians. I had to talk as though you belonged to this world or as though you were infants in the Christian life. I had to feed you with milk and not with solid food, because you couldn't handle anything stronger. And you still aren't ready (1 Corinthians 3:1,2 NLT).

Solid food is for those who are no longer infants.

3. A SWORD

A sword illustrates the power of God's Word to penetrate to the depths of our being. The writer to the Hebrews said.

> For the word of God *is* living and powerful, and sharper than any two-edged sword, piercing even to the division of soul and spirit, and of joints and marrow, and is a discerner of the thoughts and intents of the heart (Hebrews 4:12 NKJV).

The Contemporary English Version reads as follows.

> What God has said isn't only alive and active! It is sharper than any double-edged sword. His word can cut through our spirits and souls and through our joints and marrow, until it discovers the desires and thoughts of our hearts (Hebrews 4:12 CEV).

Paul emphasized the same analogy of a sword when he wrote to the church at Ephesus. He said.

> And take the helmet of salvation and the sword of the Spirit, which is the word of God (Ephesians 6:17 NET).

The sword is a powerful illustration of what the Word of God can do—it cuts to the heart.

4. FIRE AND A HAMMER

In the Book of Jeremiah, the Word of God is compared to fire and a hammer. This is how the Lord Himself describes His Word.

> "Is not My word like a fire?" says the LORD, "And like a hammer *that* breaks the rock in pieces?" (Jeremiah 23:29 NKJV).

Fire purifies, and a hammer can break something in pieces. These are some of the things that the Word of God can accomplish.

The Contemporary English Version puts it this way.

> My words are a powerful fire; they are a hammer that shatters rocks (Jeremiah 23:29 CEV).

The power of God's Word to change lives is a constant theme of Scripture.

5. A MIRROR

James uses the symbol of a mirror to illustrate the power of the Word of God. He wrote.

> Anyone who listens to the word but does not do what it says is like a man who looks at his face in a mirror and, after looking at himself, goes away and immediately forgets what he looks like. But the man who looks intently into the perfect

law that gives freedom, and continues to do this, not forgetting what he has heard, but doing it—he will be blessed in what he does (James 1:23-25 NIV).

As a mirror reflects how we look on the outside, God's Word illustrates what we look like on the inside. It reveals our true selves.

6. A SEED THAT IS SOWN

The Word of God is compared to imperishable seed that is sown. Peter wrote the following.

> For you have been born again, not of perishable seed, but of imperishable, through the living and enduring word of God (1 Peter 1:23 NIV).

Seeds that are sown bring forth life. In the same way, God's Word gives life to those who receive it. This life is imperishable—it lasts forever.

7. A LAMP AND A LIGHT

The Word of God is compared to a lamp and light. The psalmist wrote.

> Your instructions are a lamp that shows me where to walk,
> and a light that shines on my path (Psalm 119:105 NET).

His Word shows us how to walk the path of life. It keeps us on the straight and narrow road that leads to life. Jesus said.

> Enter by the narrow gate. For the gate is wide and the way is easy that leads to destruction, and those who enter by it are many. For the gate is narrow and the way is hard that leads to life, and those who find it are few (Matthew 7:13-14 ESV).

God lights the path for those who trust Him.

8. IT IS LIKE A LIGHT SHINING IN THE DARKNESS

The Bible is also compared to a light shining in the darkness. Peter wrote.

> And we have the word of the prophets made more certain, and you will do well to pay attention to it, as to a light shining in a dark place, until the day dawns and the morning star rises in your hearts (2 Peter 1:19 NIV).

As a lamp and a light guide a person through the physical darkness, God's Word guides us through the spiritual darkness.

9. WATER

The Word of God is compared to water—a necessary source of life. Paul wrote the following to the believers in Ephesus.

> Husbands, love your wives, just as Christ loved the church and gave himself up for her to make her holy, cleansing her by the washing with water through the word (Ephesians 5:25,26 NIV).

In the world of the Bible, water was very precious. The hot, dry climate created the need for saving water in every possible way. In the same manner, God's Word is both necessary and precious.

10. GOLD AND HONEY

According to the psalmist, the Scriptures are more to be desired than gold, or sweeter than the drippings of the honeycomb.

> The fear of the LORD *is* clean, enduring forever; the judgments of the LORD *are* true *and* righteous altogether. More to be desired *are they* than gold, yea, than much fine gold; sweeter also than honey and the honeycomb (Psalm 19:9,10 NKJV).

The New Living Translation says.

> Reverence for the LORD is pure, lasting forever. The laws of the LORD are true; each one is fair. They are more desirable than gold, even the finest gold. They are sweeter than honey, even honey dripping from the comb (Psalm 19:9,10 NLT).

God's Word should be sweet to us and to our taste.

11. AN ANCHOR

The Word of God is compared to an anchor. We read the following in the Book of Hebrews.

> God did this so that, by two unchangeable things in which it is impossible for God to lie, we who have fled to take hold of the hope set before us may be greatly encouraged. We have this hope as an anchor for the soul, firm and secure. It enters the inner sanctuary behind the curtain, where our forerunner, Jesus, has entered on our behalf (Hebrews 6:18-20 NIV).

An anchor speaks of security. God's Word provides security for those who rely upon it.

These word pictures, or symbols, that the Bible gives to describe itself, are very helpful in our understanding of the importance of the Word of God.

SUMMARY TO QUESTION 9
WHAT SYMBOLS OR WORD PICTURES DOES THE BIBLE USE TO DESCRIBE ITSELF?

As we examine the various symbols the Scripture uses to describe itself, we come away with a better overall understanding of it. The Bible can be compared to solid food, milk, water, honey, gold, a sword, an anchor, a mirror, a lamp and a light shining in the darkness. These different symbols provide greater insight into the character of Scripture.

QUESTION 10

What Does the Phrase, "The Word of God" Mean?

The phrase, "the Word of God" or "the Word of the Lord" has a number of different meanings in Scripture. It can mean either something that God has decreed, something that God has said when addressing humans, words that God spoke through the prophets, Jesus Christ, or finally God's written Word.

This can be illustrated as follows.

1. IT CAN BE SOMETHING THAT GOD HAS DECREED

God's decrees are His divine pronouncements. His words cause things to happen. Specifically, the Bible gives a number of examples of this. In Genesis, we read that God commands light to appear.

> In the beginning God created the heavens and the earth. Now the earth was formless and empty, darkness covered the surface of the watery depths, and the Spirit of God was hovering over the surface of the waters. Then God said, "Let there be light," and there was light (Genesis 1:1-3 HCSB).

Light comes about because of the spoken word of God. He spoke, light appeared.

When God decrees something that will, of necessity, come about, it is known as "the Word of God" or "the Word of the Lord." The psalmist wrote.

The heavens were made by the word of the Lord, and all the stars, by the breath of His mouth (Psalm 33:6 HCSB).

The New English Translation puts it this way.

By the LORD's decree the heavens were made; by a mere word from his mouth all the stars in the sky were created (Psalm 33:6 NET).

The heavens were created by the divine decrees of God.

These types of decrees were something that God desired to occur—they were not necessarily spoken to anyone. Yet, they are called "the Word of God" or "the Word of the Lord." Indeed, the universe is upheld by the Word of God. The writer to the Hebrews said.

The Son is the radiance of God's glory and the exact representation of his being, sustaining all things by his powerful word (Hebrews 1:3 NIV).

Therefore, God's divine speech causes certain events to happen, and on some occasions, causes things to come into being. His divine decrees caused the universe to come about. and it allows the universe to continue to exist.

2. IT MAY REFER TO GOD VERBALLY ADDRESSING HUMANS: A PERSONAL ADDRESS

When God verbally addressed certain humans in the past, His words were known as the Word of God. Scripture gives a number of illustrations of God addressing humans in human language. For example, God personally spoke to Adam in the Garden of Eden.

And the LORD God commanded the man, "You may freely eat of every tree of the garden; but of the tree of the knowledge of good and evil you shall not eat, for in the day that you eat of it you shall die" (Genesis 2:16-17 NRSV).

Thus, the phrase "the Word of God," or the "Word of the Lord" can refer to the actual words God used in speaking to humans in their own language. This type of personal address from God is found throughout Scripture.

When the Ten Commandments were given, God personally spoke them to Moses. The Bible says.

> And God spoke all these words, saying, "I am the Lord your God, who brought you out of the land of Egypt, out of the house of slavery. "You shall have no other gods before me" (Exodus 20:1-3 ESV).

Therefore, the Word of God may refer to the actual words that God spoke to humans. In these instances, the people were hearing the very voice of the living God. His words were completely understandable— spoken in ordinary human language. The people were expected to obey these words that God had spoken.

3. IT CAN REFER TO GOD SPEAKING THROUGH HUMAN PROPHETS

The phrase "Word of God" is also used of something that is said by God's chosen spokesmen. The Bible says that God spoke to His people through the words of the prophets. These words consisted of ordinary language spoken through human beings.

When the biblical prophets spoke for the Lord, their words were called the "Word of God." The Lord promised that the prophets would speak His words. He said to Moses.

> I will raise up a prophet like you for them from among their fellow Israelites. I will put my words in his mouth and he will speak to them whatever I want. I myself will hold responsible anyone who then pays no attention to the words that prophet will speak in my name. But any prophet who presumes to speak anything in my name that I have not authorized him

to speak, or who speaks in the name of other gods—that prophet must die (Deuteronomy 18:18-20 NET).

While the words of the prophets were the speech of human beings, they carried God's divine authority. The words spoken by God's prophets were supposed to be obeyed. However, those who falsely claimed to speak God's word were to be punished.

In another instance, the Lord promised to tell the prophet Jeremiah what to say to the people. The Bible says.

> The LORD said to me, "Do not say, 'I am too young.' But go to whomever I send you and say whatever I tell you" (Jeremiah 1:7 NET).

The Lord assured Jeremiah that his words to the people would be God's words. We also read in Jeremiah.

> Then the LORD reached out his hand and touched my mouth and said to me, "I will most assuredly give you the words you are to speak for me" (Jeremiah 1:9 NET).

Scripture makes no distinction in the authority of the words that God directly spoke, and those things that were spoken by His prophets. Everything that was said was considered to be the Word of God because God was their ultimate source. God used ordinary human beings and spoke through them in their own language to communicate the Word of God. Consequently, the words were to be obeyed.

We must note that while God did personally speak to humans, or used humans as His personal spokesmen, these occurrences were rare—they were not the norm. This was not the way in which He regularly communicated with humanity.

4. JESUS CHRIST IS THE WORD OF GOD

God the Son, Jesus Christ, is known as the Word of God. At the beginning of John's gospel we read the following.

In the beginning was the Word, and the Word was with God, and the Word was God (John 1:1 KJV).

In the Book of Revelation, John describes the risen Christ as the "Word of God." He wrote.

He is clothed in a robe dipped in blood, and the name by which he is called is The Word of God (Revelation 19:13 ESV).

The New Living Translation says.

He was clothed with a robe dipped in blood, and his title was the Word of God (Revelation 19:13 NLT).

This description, the Word of God, is only used for God the Son—it is not used for God the Father or God the Holy Spirit. God the Son, Jesus Christ, is the one member of the Trinity who personally communicated God to humanity. However, since there are only two references in the New Testament that refer to Jesus Christ as the Word of God, this usage is rare.

5. IT ALSO REFERS TO GOD'S WRITTEN WORD

Finally, the "Word of God" can refer to God's Word in written form— the Bible. After being proclaimed orally, God's Word was put into written form. Moses was told to write down God's words.

Then the LORD said to Moses, "Write this on a scroll as something to be remembered and make sure that Joshua hears it, because I will completely blot out the memory of Amalek from under heaven" (Exodus 17:14 NIV).

Elsewhere, we again read about God telling Moses to write something down.

> And the Lord said to Moses, "Write these words, for in accordance with these words I have made a covenant with you and with Israel" (Exodus 34:27 ESV).

In the New Testament, Jesus contrasted the written Word of God with the ungodly tradition of the people. He said.

> But you say, 'If someone tells his father or mother, "Whatever help you would have received from me is given to God," he certainly does not honor his father.' You have nullified the word of God on account of your tradition (Matthew 15:5,6 NET).

According to Jesus, these human-made traditions nullified the Word of God. The written Word of God, the Hebrew Scripture, was the only source of authority for the people until Jesus came. While these were human words, they still carried God's divine authority.

The New Testament appears to use the terms "Word of God," Word of the Lord," and "Word of Christ" interchangeably. All of them refer to God's authoritative Word.

Therefore, we find that the Scripture uses the phrase "the Word of God" in five distinct ways—God's divine decrees, God personally speaking to people in their language, the words of God's divinely inspired prophets, Jesus Christ, and the written Word of God. The context must determine how the phrase is to be understood.

SUMMARY TO QUESTION 10
WHAT DOES THE PHRASE, "THE WORD OF GOD" MEAN?

The phrase, "the Word of God" is used in a number of different ways. It refers to something that God has decreed to come to pass. It is also used of the actual spoken words of God. Words that God has spoken through the prophets can also be called "the Word of God. Jesus Christ Himself is called the Word of God. Finally, the phrase can also refer to God's written Word.

The words that were delivered by God's designated spokesmen, the prophets, as well as the written Word of God, though not as dramatic, carried the same authority as the actual words spoken by God.

While all five ways that God has spoken to humanity can be called the "Word of God," the only form available for us to study is the written Scripture. Indeed, we would not know about the other four areas of God's Word except for His written Word—the Bible.

Does the Old Testament Claim to be the Word of God?

Throughout its history, the Christian church has believed and taught that the Bible, in both testaments, is the Word of God. It alone is the written communication of God to humanity. The church has not invented this claim—it is the claim of the Bible itself. The evidence for the Old Testament being the Word of God is as follows.

1. THE CLAIMS FOUND IN THE OLD TESTAMENT

We find in the Old Testament the claim that the words and deeds it records come from the living God. In thousands of passages, it plainly declares to be the very Word of the living God. In fact, over five thousand times the Old Testament declares, "God said," or "Thus says the Lord."

2. THE IMPORTANCE OF "THUS SAYS THE LORD"

The phrase, "Thus says the Lord," is extremely important. It has the same wording as the phrase, "Thus says the King." In the ancient world, this phrase prefaced an edict, or command, that a king would make to his subjects. Such commands had to be obeyed by the people—they could not be challenged.

The fact that the Old Testament prophets used this specific introduction to their words shows they claimed to be the spokesmen for the

Lord. As spokesmen, their words would have the absolute authority of the Lord behind them. They had to be obeyed and they could not be challenged. This shows the importance of the Bible using such a phrase. God's Word must be obeyed and should never be challenged.

WHAT THE OLD TESTAMENT SAYS ABOUT ITSELF

There are a number of things that the Old Testament has to say about itself. They include the following.

1. THE AUTHORS RECORDED GOD'S ACTUAL WORDS

Many times, we are told the Old Testament authors recorded the words that the Lord had spoken. Moses wrote.

> Aaron told them [Pharaoh's magicians] everything the LORD had told Moses, and Moses performed the miraculous signs as they watched (Exodus 4:30 NLT).

In the Book of Joshua, we read about Joshua commanding the people to hear God's Words. The Bible says.

> So Joshua said to the children of Israel, "Come here, and hear the words of the LORD your God" (Joshua 3:9 NKJV).

We read in the Book of Second Kings how the Word of the Lord was given to the people of Israel. It says.

> The LORD solemnly warned Israel and Judah through all his prophets and all the seers, "Turn back from your evil ways; obey my commandments and rules that are recorded in the law. I ordered your ancestors to keep this law and sent my servants the prophets to remind you of its demands" (2 Kings 17:13 NET).

The prophet Isaiah testified to a particular decree that God had made. He wrote.

Carefully read the scroll of the LORD! Not one of these crea-
tures will be missing, none will lack a mate. For the LORD
has issued the decree, and his personal spirit gathers them
(Isaiah 34:16 NET).

Therefore, on numerous occasions, the Old Testament claims to records
the very words that God spoke.

2. THE PROPHETS SPOKE GOD'S ACTUAL WORDS

On other occasions, the words recorded were from God's designated
spokesmen. These words would have the same authority as the direct
words from God. We read of God speaking through the prophet Ahijah.

They buried him, and all Israel mourned for him, as the
LORD had said through his servant the prophet Ahijah
(1 Kings 14:18 NIV).

We also read of the authority of the earlier prophets. Zechariah wrote
about this. He said.

Were not these the words that the LORD proclaimed by the
former prophets, when Jerusalem was inhabited and in prosperity, along with the towns around it, and when the Negeb
and the Shephelah were inhabited? (Zechariah 7:7 NRSV).

These specially designated spokesmen for the Lord delivered God's
Word with the authority of the Lord. Their words were expected to be
obeyed.

3. THE REVEALED WORD OF GOD WILL BENEFIT FUTURE GENERATIONS

These words which God spoke, as well as the words spoken through
His specially chosen spokesmen, were recorded for the benefit of future
generations. The Scripture says the following.

> "And as for me, this is my covenant with them," says the Lord: "My Spirit that is upon you, and my words that I have put in your mouth, shall not depart out of your mouth, or out of the mouth of your offspring, or out of the mouth of your children's offspring," says the Lord, "from this time forth and forevermore" (Isaiah 59:21 ESV).

The words of God, as given in the Old Testament, were meant to be passed on to others. They were not merely for those who originally heard it.

4. GOD'S WORDS ARE INFALLIBLE

The words of God, as recorded in the Old Testament, are an infallible guide to humanity. When God promised something, it came to pass. Moses wrote.

> God is not a man, that he should lie. He is not a human, that he should change his mind. Has he ever spoken and failed to act? Has he ever promised and not carried it through? (Numbers 23:19 NLT).

God's Word does not lie. The words recorded in the Old Testament are God's infallible words.

5. GOD'S WORDS ARE ETERNAL AND UNCHANGING

The Word of God, as revealed in the Old Testament, is eternal and unchanging. Isaiah the prophet wrote about how God's Word will last forever.

> The grass withers, the flower fades, but the word of our God stands forever (Isaiah 40:8 NKJV).

The psalmist also emphasized that the words of God are secure in the heavens—they will not be changed in any manner. He wrote.

O LORD, your instructions endure; they stand secure in heaven (Psalm 119:89 NET).

The fact that God's Word is forever settled is a comforting truth for believers.

6. HIS WORDS ARE POWERFUL

The Old Testament also says that God's Word is powerful. Jeremiah recorded the Lord making the following comparison of His words to fire and a hammer.

"Is not my word like fire," declares the LORD, "and like a hammer that breaks a rock in pieces?" (Jeremiah 23:29 NKJV).

God's Words get results because of their divine power.

7. GOD'S WORDS ARE TRUE

The Old Testament records things that are true, or trustworthy. The psalmist wrote.

The law of the LORD is perfect, reviving the soul. The statutes of the LORD are trustworthy, making wise the simple (Psalm 19:7 NIV).

The psalmist elsewhere emphasized the reliability of the words of God. He said.

Your justice endures, and your law is reliable (Psalm 119:142 NET).

Through the prophet Isaiah, the Lord said that His words accomplish the purpose for which they were given.

In the same way, the promise that I make does not return to me, having accomplished nothing. No, it is realized as I desire and is fulfilled as I intend (Isaiah 55:11 NET).

The true Word of God will always accomplish its divine purpose. These are the claims of the Old Testament.

8. GOD'S WORDS ARE A GUIDE FOR DAILY LIVING

The Old Testament is a guide for living a godly life. The psalmist proclaimed.

> Your instructions are a lamp that shows me where to walk,
> and a light that shines on my path (Psalm 119:105 NET).

In Proverbs, we read about how God's Word helps us with our daily lives. It says.

> For the commandments are like a lamp, instruction is like a
> light, and rebukes of discipline are like the road leading to
> life (Proverbs 6:23 NET).

Therefore, His Word, as recorded in the Old Testament, is extremely practical.

9. WE ARE NOT TO ADD OR SUBTRACT TO GOD'S WORD

Because the Old Testament is the Word of the Lord, people were commanded not to add to it, or subtract from it. The Lord said.

> You must be careful to do everything I am commanding you.
> Do not add to it or subtract from it! (Deuteronomy 12:32
> NET).

Since God's words are of the highest importance to Him no one was allowed to tamper with them.

CONCLUSION: THE OLD TESTAMENT CLAIMS TO BE GOD'S WORD TO HUMANITY

These are a number of the things the Old Testament says about itself. It is clear from its contents that the Old Testament claims divine authority. It claims to record the very words of the living God. It is important to realize that this is the claim of the Old Testament itself—it is not something that someone else has said about it. Consequently, these claims must be taken seriously.

SUMMARY TO QUESTION 11
DOES THE OLD TESTAMENT CLAIM TO BE THE WORD OF GOD?

From the statements contained in the Old Testament, we can see that it claims to record the words and deeds of the living God. We also observe that the statements made about God's Word assure us that humanity can place their trust in His promises. Furthermore, the Old Testament commands were expected to be obeyed.

Again, we emphasize that this is the claim of the Old Testament itself. Therefore, the claims should be weighed and evaluated.

How Does the New Testament View the Old Testament?

The Old Testament claimed to record God's Word to humanity. The New Testament writers also believed that the Old Testament was God's divine revelation to the human race. We discover this in a number of ways.

1. THE OLD TESTAMENT IS CITED WITH FORMULAS SUCH AS "IT IS WRITTEN" OR "GOD SAID"

In the New Testament, the Old Testament is cited with the formulas such as, "it is written," "God says," or "the Holy Spirit says." We read in the Book of Acts that David, the human writer, spoke through the Holy Spirit. The Bible says.

> And when they heard it, they lifted their voices together to God and said, "Sovereign Lord, who made the heaven and the earth and the sea and everything in them, who through the mouth of our father David, your servant, said by the Holy Spirit, "Why did the Gentiles rage, and the peoples plot in vain?" (Acts 4:24,25 ESV).

This is a quotation from Psalm 2:1-2. From this passage, we discover that the early church believed the Holy Spirit had spoken through David.

The Apostle Paul, in referring to the Old Testament, said the Lord has made certain commands. We read Paul's words in the Book of Acts.

> For so the Lord has commanded us, saying, "I have made you a light for the Gentiles, that you may bring salvation to the ends of the earth" (Acts 13:47 ESV).

Here Paul is alluding to Isaiah 42:6 and 49:6. Again, the words of the Old Testament were God's words.

In another place, Paul refers to the Old Testament and states that, "God said." We read the following in Second Corinthians.

> What agreement has the temple of God with idols? For we are the temple of the living God; as God said, "I will make my dwelling among them and walk among them, and I will be their God, and they shall be my people" (2 Corinthians 6:16 ESV).

This is a quotation from Leviticus 26:12. Therefore, we find that the Old Testament is treated as Scripture by the writers of the New Testament by the use of these formulas.

2. THE TERMS "GOD" AND "OLD TESTAMENT SCRIPTURE" WERE USED INTERCHANGEABLY

The word "God" and the words "Old Testament Scripture" are closely joined together in the New Testament. In fact, the writers speak of Scripture doing something that God is doing. We see the following examples of God and Scripture used interchangeably.

In the Book of Genesis, it says that God called Abraham.

> Now the LORD said to Abram, "Go from your country and your kindred and your father's house to the land that I will show you. I will make of you a great nation, and I will bless you, and make your name great, so that you will be a

blessing. I will bless those who bless you, and the one who curses you I will curse; and in you all the families of the earth shall be blessed" (Genesis 12:1-3 NRSV).

Yet in the New Testament, it attributes these words to Scripture, not God. Paul wrote.

And the Scripture, foreseeing that God would justify the Gentiles by faith, preached the gospel beforehand to Abraham, saying, "In you shall all the nations be blessed" (Galatians 3:8 ESV).

In the Old Testament, it says that the Lord spoke to Pharaoh. It records the Lord saying the following.

But this is why I have let you live: to show you my power, and to make my name resound through all the earth (Exodus 9:16 NRSV).

While the Old Testament records that the Lord spoke to Pharaoh, the New Testament says, "Scripture says to Pharaoh." We read the following in Paul's letter to the Romans.

For the Scripture says to Pharaoh, "For this very purpose I have raised you up, that I might show my power in you, and that my name might be proclaimed in all the earth" (Romans 9:17 ESV).

Again, we have Scripture and the Lord used interchangeably. This shows the New Testament writers viewed the Old Testament as the absolutely authoritative Word of God.

3. THE NEW TESTAMENT ATTRIBUTES ANONYMOUS OLD TESTAMENT STATEMENTS TO GOD AND THE HOLY SPIRIT

There are a number of statements found in the Old Testament where the speaker is not identified but the New Testament attributes them to either God, or to the Holy Spirit.

For example, the Old Testament records the following statement in the Book of Psalms without mentioning the speaker. It says the following.

> Today, if you hear his voice, do not harden your hearts as you did at Meribah, as you did that day at Massah in the desert (Psalm 95:7,8 NRSV).

While the speaker is not identified in the Old Testament, the New Testament attributes this statement to the Holy Spirit. We read.

> Therefore, as the Holy Spirit says, "Today, if you hear his voice" (Hebrews 3:7 NRSV).

The Second Psalm records the following statements without identifying the speaker.

> Why do the nations conspire and the peoples plot in vain? The kings of the earth take their stand and the rulers gather together against the LORD and against his Anointed One (Psalm 2:1,2 NIV).

In the New Testament, these words are attributed to the Holy Spirit through the mouth of David. It says.

> It is you who said by the Holy Spirit through our ancestor David, your servant: 'Why did the Gentiles rage, and the peoples imagine vain things? The kings of the earth took their stand, and the rulers have gathered together against the Lord and against his Messiah' (Acts 4:24,25 NRSV).

In the Old Testament, we read the following promise without the speaker being identified.

> Give ear and come to me; hear me, that your soul may live. I will make an everlasting covenant with you, my faithful love promised to David (Isaiah 55:3 NIV).

The New Testament identifies God as the one who made the promise. We read of the Apostle Paul saying the following.

> God raised him from the dead so that he will never be subject to decay. As God has said, "I will give you the holy and sure blessings promised to David" (Acts 13:34 NIV).

Again, we find an anonymous Old Testament statement attributed to God in the New Testament.

CONCLUSION: THE NEW TESTAMENT VIEWS THE OLD TESTAMENT AS THE WORD OF GOD

These passages are further indication that the New Testament writers believed the Old Testament was God's Word. Of this, there is no doubt. Therefore, the consistent teaching of the New Testament is that the Old Testament is the Word of the Living God.

SUMMARY TO QUESTION 12
HOW DOES THE NEW TESTAMENT VIEW THE OLD TESTAMENT?

The Old Testament writers unanimously taught that the Old Testament is the Word of the Lord. To begin with, the Old Testament is directly cited as being the God's Word.

In addition, we find statements in the Old Testament attributed to the Lord which the New Testament attributes to Scripture.

We also find statements in the Old Testament that are not attributed to anyone that the New Testament attributes to either God or the Holy Spirit. Consequently, God and Scripture are used interchangeably.

Consequently, there is no doubt that the New Testament writers considered the Old Testament to be God's Word.

Does the New Testament Claim to be the Word of God?

God's revelation to humanity was not finished with the Old Testament. The New Testament also claims to be God Word to the human race. The evidence is as follows.

1. JESUS' WORDS WERE GIVEN BY GOD THE FATHER

When Jesus prayed to God the Father on the night that He was betrayed, He said that His words were the words that God the Father had given Him. He said.

> For I gave them the words you gave me and they accepted them. They knew with certainty that I came from you, and they believed that you sent me (John 17:8 NIV).

Thus, Jesus testified to the divine origin of His Words. The consistent theme in the ministry of Jesus was that His words were actually the words of God the Father. There is something else. These words were accepted as true by Jesus' apostles. They believed that the words of Jesus were the words of God.

2. THE WORDS OF JESUS WERE TRUE

Jesus also affirmed that God's Word is true in all that it says. As He was about to be betrayed, He prayed to God the Father.

> Set them apart in the truth; your word is truth (John 17:17 NET).

His words were always true.

3. JESUS' WORDS ARE ETERNAL

Jesus said His words were everlasting: He made the incredible claim that His words would never pass away. He said.

> Heaven and earth shall pass away, but my words shall not pass away (Matthew 24:35 KJV).

It is interesting to note that His claim has been literally fulfilled—His words are still with us to this day.

4. JESUS SAID THERE WERE MORE AUTHORITATIVE WORDS TO COME

Jesus stated plainly that more revelation was to come after He left this world. On the night of His betrayal, He said the following to His disciples.

> I have much more to say to you, more than you can now bear (John 16:12 NIV).

From this statement we discover that Jesus would leave unfinished the revelation of God's truth to humanity. This opened the door for God to reveal a "New" Testament to the world.

5. GOD'S WORD WAS GIVEN THROUGH HUMAN BEINGS

As was true with the Old Testament, God's Word was conveyed through human instrumentation, but not through human wisdom. Paul wrote.

> And we speak of these things in words not taught by human wisdom but taught by the Spirit, interpreting spiritual things to those who are spiritual (1 Corinthians 2:13 NRSV).

The New King James Version reads.

> These things we also speak, not in words which man's wisdom teaches but which the Holy Spirit teaches, comparing spiritual things with spiritual (1 Corinthians 2:13 NKJV).

God used humans to convey His words.

6. THE WORDS OF THE NEW TESTAMENT WRITERS ARE THE WORDS OF GOD

The New Testament, like the Old Testament, claims to record the words of God. In what was probably the earliest letter of the Apostle Paul to a church, he wrote the following.

> We also constantly give thanks to God for this, that when you received the word of God that you heard from us, you accepted it not as a human word but as what it really is, God's word, which is also at work in you believers (1 Thessalonians 2:13 NRSV).

The words of Paul are equated with the words of God.

7. GOD'S WORDS THROUGH THE WRITERS ARE AUTHORITATIVE

The Word of God, as recorded in the New Testament, is presented as the final authority on all matters in which it speaks. Jesus said the following about His own words.

> It is the Spirit who gives life; the flesh profits nothing. The words that I speak to you are spirit, and *they* are life (John 6:63 NKJV).

Simon Peter acknowledged that only Jesus had the words of eternal life. John records him saying the following.

But Simon Peter answered Him, "Lord, to whom shall we go? You have the words of eternal life" (John 6:68 NKJV).

The words of Jesus carried ultimate authority.

8. GOD'S WORDS ARE EXPECTED TO BE OBEYED

When certain people spoke the words of God, the Scripture tells us that the people were expected to obey their words. The words in which they spoke were ultimately God's Words—He was the source of what they said. Paul wrote.

> If anyone thinks himself to be a prophet or spiritual, let him acknowledge that the things which I write to you are the commandments of the Lord (1 Corinthians 14:37 NKJV).

Because they were God's words, they carried His divine authority.

CONCLUSION: THE NEW TESTAMENT IS GOD'S WORD

Like the Old Testament, the New Testament claims to record the Word of God to humanity. This is the clear teaching of each of the two testaments—it is not something that the church later decided. This being the case, the claims made need to be taken seriously.

THE STATEMENT THE BIBLE IS GOD'S WORD NEEDS TO BE CLARIFIED

There is a clarification that we need to make. When we say that Bible is the Word of God, it does not mean that God spoke everything that is recorded in its pages. The Bible also contains the words of hundreds of different men and women. What the Bible claims for itself is that it is a true account of what these people actually said. Those people who were speaking for God had God's authority behind their words.

However some individuals, who did not speak for God, also had their words recorded. While their words are part of Holy Scripture, they do not have God's divine authority behind them. Their words are not to be understood as infallible truth from God. The context makes it clear whether a person is speaking for God, or that Scripture is merely recording the non-authoritative words of someone. It is crucial that we make this distinction.

SUMMARY TO QUESTION 13
DOES THE NEW TESTAMENT CLAIM TO BE THE WORD OF GOD?

It is clear that the New Testament, by direct statements, testifies to its own divine origin and unique authority. The New Testament claims to be God's revealed Word to humanity. It claims the following things: it is a record of God speaking, it is infallible, it was written to benefit future generations, it is eternal and unchanging, it is powerful, true, a guide for daily living, authoritative, and the Word of God. Thus, it is the assertion of Scripture itself that it is more than a mere human book—it is the very Word of God. These claims must be taken seriously.

However, not every word in the Bible was spoken from God. Scripture records the speech of hundreds of different people. Some of them spoke for God, and some of them said things that were contrary to the truth of God. The context must determine whether something in Scripture is a Word from God, or the mere words of humans.

How Do We Know the Bible Is the Word of God?

In both testaments, the Bible claims to be God's communication to humanity—the only divine revelation from the one true God. But is this claim true? How do we know the Bible is what is claims to be—the Word of God?

THERE ARE TWO BASIC APPROACHES TO THIS QUESTION

There are two different approaches that are taken when it comes to arguing for the Bible to be the Word of God. First, there are those who believe that the Scripture is self-authenticating. The Bible is true because it says it is true, and the Holy Spirit bears witness to this truth. No other argument is necessary.

A second approach believes that the claims of Scripture have sufficient evidence to back them up. Those who hold this view believe there is overwhelming evidence to convince anyone that the Bible is what it claims to be—the Word of God. People, therefore, need to check out the evidence—not merely blindly believe the claims of Scripture.

We can summarize the two approaches as follows.

APPROACH 1: THE BIBLE IS SELF-AUTHENTICATING

To many people, the issue of the Bible's authority is something that should not be debated. The authority of the Bible must be believed because the Scripture says so. This is usually argued in the following ways.

THE BIBLE CLAIMS TO BE GOD'S WORD: NO OTHER TESTIMONY IS NECESSARY

The Bible should be allowed to speak for itself. It clearly claims to be God's Word. It doesn't need defending. If we attempt to defend the Bible, then we are placing some other standard as the ultimate judge. Whether it is scientific or historical accuracy, human reasoning, or some other standard, what we are doing is placing Scripture under that standard. What Scripture says should be our ultimate standard, and everything should be judged by its claims—it should be judged by no one.

There is something else. The problem with providing evidence for the Bible is that human beings are both sinful and finite. They must still evaluate any evidence offered for the truthfulness of the Christian faith. Again, it places some sort of human standard as the final authority. Evidence gathered from other sources may be useful, but it has nothing convincing to say about the truth of Christianity.

THE BIBLE SHOULD BE ABLE TO TESTIFY ON ITS OWN BEHALF

In a court of law people have a right to testify on their own behalf. Since the Bible is the Word of God, the author, God, should be allowed to testify what sort of Book the Bible is. This is particularly true because the Bible says that God cannot lie. His testimony should be received as final.

THE WITNESS OF THE HOLY SPIRIT DEMONSTRATES THE TRUTHFULNESS OF SCRIPTURE

However, the Bible does more than merely claim to be God's Word. The witness of the Spirit shows the reader that the Bible is the Word of God. When the truths of the Bible are personally applied, the credibility of the Bible is demonstrated. Paul wrote.

You yourselves are our letter, written on our hearts, to be known and read by all (2 Corinthians 3:2 NRSV).

Paul said that people would see the truths of the Word of God at work in the lives of God's people. This was its testimony. When the truths are lived out in one's life, we find that they work.

As people read the Bible, they find the Holy Spirit giving confirmation that what they are reading is God's Word. Therefore, we not only have the claim of Scripture, we also have the witness of the Holy Spirit that the things written in Scripture are true.

OBJECTION: THIS IS ARGUING IN A CIRCLE: ASSUMING WHAT YOU SHOULD BE PROVING

Those who criticize this approach say that it is circular reasoning—it is assuming what it should be proving. Quoting the Bible to prove the Bible, does not prove anything. Why should the claims of the Bible be believed? There are many religious books that claim to convey truth. In addition, adherents can be found who will testify as to the power of the truths in these books to change their lives. How can anyone know which claims, if any of them, are right and which claims are wrong? Religious experience alone is not a valid test. Something else is needed.

APPROACH 2: EXAMINE THE EVIDENCE THAT GOD HAS GIVEN

A second approach to the truth of the Bible's claims is to examine the evidence about the truthfulness of Christianity. The Bible's claim to authority is not in-and-of-itself proof of its divine authority. Arguing that the claims of the Bible are more persuasive than the claims of all other religious writings does not always work in real life. There will be those who are not convinced of the Bible's claims. What should we do with these people? Should they be ignored?

THERE ARE THREE LINES OF EVIDENCE FOR THE TRUTH OF JESUS' CLAIMS: MIRACLES, FULFILLED PROPHECY, AND HIS RESURRECTION

The Bible never argues for the existence of God—it takes this for granted. But the New Testament does argue about the truth of the claims of Jesus through three lines of evidence. The evidence consists of miracles, fulfilled prophecy, and the resurrection of Jesus Christ from the dead. When the evidence is considered, the verdict becomes clear that Jesus is whom He claimed to be.

WE SHOULD DO WHAT JESUS' FOLLOWERS DID: EMPHASIZE THESE THREE AREAS OF EVIDENCE

There is another important point to make. Because the claims of Scripture, on their own, do not constitute any type of convincing proof, we should argue the same way in which Jesus' disciples argued. They presented compelling proof to the people that Jesus was the Christ.

For example, on the Day of Pentecost, Peter stated the following evidence to the large crowd that had gathered.

> You that are Israelites, listen to what I have to say: Jesus of Nazareth, a man attested to you by God with deeds of power, wonders, and signs that God did through him among you, as you yourselves know-- this man, handed over to you according to the definite plan and foreknowledge of God, you crucified and killed by the hands of those outside the law. But God raised him up, having freed him from death, because it was impossible for him to be held in its power. For David says concerning him, 'I saw the Lord always before me, for he is at my right hand so that I will not be shaken; therefore my heart was glad, and my tongue rejoiced; moreover my flesh will live in hope. For you will not abandon my soul to Hades, or let your Holy One experience corruption. You have made known to me the ways of life; you will make me full of gladness with your presence' (Acts 2:22-28 NRSV).

In this one passage, we find Peter appealing to these three different lines of evidence.

First, he spoke of the miracles of Jesus Christ—it was something that the entire crowd was aware of.

He also testified to the fact that Jesus came back from the dead—something to which Peter and the other disciples were witnesses.

Finally, Peter said that Jesus' resurrection was a fulfillment of Bible prophecy.

Therefore, he appealed to miracles, Jesus' resurrection, and fulfilled prophecy to convince the people that Jesus was indeed "the Christ."

We also find that the Apostle Paul reasoned with unbelievers from the Scriptures. In the Book of Acts, we read the following.

> Then Paul, as his custom was, went in to them, and for three Sabbaths reasoned with them from the Scriptures, explaining and demonstrating that the Christ had to suffer and rise again from the dead, and saying, "This Jesus whom I preach to you is the Christ" (Acts 17:2,3 NKJV).

Since this is the way that the New Testament believers reasoned with unbelievers about the claims of Jesus Christ, we should do the same when it comes to the authority of the Bible. Therefore, we should not limit ourselves to merely citing the Bible to prove the Bible.

ULTIMATELY, WE MUST TASTE AND FOR OURSELVES

A person can know the Bible is God's Word by first examining the claims of Scripture, considering the evidence for those claims, and then personally accepting the challenge of Scripture to "taste and see" if these things be true. The psalmist gave the following challenge.

Oh, taste and see that the LORD *is* good; blessed *is* the man *who* trusts in Him! (Psalm 34:8 NKJV).

The New Revised Standard Version says.

O taste and see that the LORD is good; happy are those who take refuge in him (Psalm 34:8 NRSV).

Ultimately, a person must individually experience the truth of God's Word for themselves. This occurs by coming to God in faith and then believing in His promises.

SUMMARY TO QUESTION 14
HOW DO WE KNOW THE BIBLE IS THE WORD OF GOD?

While the Bible claims to be the authoritative Word of God there have been two basic approaches as to how anyone can know these claims are true.

One approach believes that the Bible should be taken at its Word and not defended. The Holy Spirit will show the truth of its claim to anyone who is interested in knowing. Nothing else is necessary. This way the Bible is not made subject to any other type of authority.

On the other hand, there are those who point to evidences that God has provided to argue for the truth of Scripture. These include miracles, fulfilled prophecy, and Jesus' resurrection from the dead. Taken together they constitute overwhelming evidence for the truth of God's Word. Christians employ both methods in defending and proclaiming Scripture.

However, merely knowing intellectually that the Bible is God's Word is not enough. The Bible says that we need to personally experience the God of the Bible by believing in His promises and submitting to His commands.

Why Do We Need A Written Revelation from God?

There are a number of ways in which God could have chosen to reveal Himself to humanity. These include the following: God could have personally revealed Himself to everyone; He could have had His Word passed on by oral communication, or He could have had His Word committed to writing. The following observations need to be made about this subject.

A PERSONAL REVELATION TO EACH INDIVIDUAL IS NOT PRACTICAL

God could have chosen to personally reveal Himself to each individual, yet He did not. There would have been insurmountable problems if He had chosen this way. They include the following.

1. NOT EVERYONE WOULD BE WILLING TO RECEIVE GOD'S MESSAGE

First, not everyone would be willing to receive what God wanted to say. Some people would have to be forced to receive God's personal revelation to them. They simply would not want to hear it.

The Bible says that God does not force anyone to receive His message. Jesus compared His desire to talk to people to knocking at a door. He said.

> Behold, I stand at the door and knock. If anyone hears my voice and opens the door, I will come in to him and eat with him, and he with me (Revelation 3:20 ESV).

To hear His voice, people must open the door—He will not break down the door.

2. THE SAME MESSAGE WOULD HAVE TO BE CONTINUOUSLY REPEATED

If God personally revealed Himself to everyone, then He would have had to have repeated the same message over and over again to each of us. This would seemingly be a waste of time and effort. Why go to all that trouble when there is a much simpler way?

3. PERSONAL REVELATION WOULD ONLY CAUSE MORE CONFUSION

Finally, this method would only lead to confusion. People would not agree with each other as to what God had revealed to them. This being the case, then the question would be, "Who would decide which person had the correct revelation from God?" Obviously, some other method of God revealing Himself to humanity is necessary.

4. ORAL COMMUNICATION IS NOT A SATISFACTORY SOLUTION

There is also the possibility that God's Word could have been passed along simply by oral communication. The people to whom God spoke would verbally pass on His Word to others. However, oral communication has the following problems.

A NON-WRITTEN MESSAGE COULD BE CHANGED

First, if we were given only an oral communication from God, then we would have a message that could be changed and misinterpreted when repeatedly told. Memory and tradition are untrustworthy guides. The more the story was repeated orally, the more the story could be changed. This would not give us much confidence in the message.

THERE WOULD BE NO AGREEMENT AS TO WHICH VERSION SHOULD BE TRUSTED

Moreover, if the message began to differ considerably, how would anyone know which version to trust? A revelation from God based upon oral communication would be beset with many problems. It would soon be more confusion than help.

SINFUL HUMANITY, ON THEIR OWN, IS NOT CAPABLE OF DOING THIS

Finally, sinful humanity, left to themselves, is incapable of correctly passing along an infallible oral communication over an extended period of time. Our sinful and limited natures would keep us from accurately and truthfully passing on God's Word by transmitting it orally. Something else is needed.

A WRITTEN REVELATION IS ABSOLUTELY NECESSARY FOR A NUMBER OF REASONS

Consequently, there are a number of reasons why a written revelation from God to humanity is absolutely necessary. They are as follows.

1. THE IMPORTANCE OF THE SUBJECT DEMANDS IT

First, the importance of the subject necessitates a revelation from God being put into writing. Because the eternal destiny of every human being hangs upon a proper response to God's revelation, it becomes absolutely essential that it be written down. Because it has been committed to writing, it has been made public for all to see. This makes it more accessible.

2. THE WRITTEN MESSAGE CAN BE ACCURATELY PRESERVED FOR FUTURE GENERATIONS

Once the words and deeds have been committed to writing, the message can be preserved. This allows succeeding generations to have the benefit of seeing what the original writers said. Thus, the written Word of God makes His truth available to many more people. By putting the messages in a book, such as the Bible, the truth can be preserved for future generations. God continues to speak—though the people who originally gave the messages, as well as those who first received the messages, have died. Therefore, the truths of Scripture would be an infallible standard for all people of all ages.

We note that God commanded the prophet Isaiah to write down His words to preserve them for future generations. The Lord said.

> Now go, write it down on a tablet in their presence, inscribe it on a scroll, so that it might be saved for a future time as an enduring witness (Isaiah 30:8 NET).

The words could forever be preserved. The writer's die—but their writings live on.

3. A WRITTEN MESSAGE CAN SOLVE DOCTRINAL ISSUES

A written revelation also solves doctrinal controversies. If there is a question concerning Christian belief, the written Bible can be studied as an authoritative source to solve the problem. Therefore, all questions have a final source of authority in which to resolve them.

In Jesus' day when a religious question came up, the people immediately went to the Old Testament Scripture to find their answer. For example, when King Herod heard that the Christ had been born, he went to the religious leaders to find out where. They found the answer to this question in the Scriptures. The Bible says.

> When King Herod heard this he was alarmed, and all Jerusalem with him. After assembling all the chief priests and experts in the law he asked them where the Christ was to be born. "In Bethlehem of Judea," they said, "for it is written this way by the prophet" (Matthew 2:3-5 NET).

When the Scriptures were cited, this solved the question once-and-for-all. Humanity has an authoritative basis to go to find ultimate answers.

4. A WRITTEN MESSAGE CAN BE EXAMINED REPEATEDLY

Once God's Word had been put into written form, it can be examined time and time again. It is available for discussion, as well as for careful study.

Indeed, it can be publicly and privately examined by believers and unbelievers alike. It provides the basis for discussion of its contents. Therefore, it is a message that is available to all—not to just a select few.

5. A WRITTEN MESSAGE CAN BE TRANSLATED ACCURATELY INTO OTHER LANGUAGES

Once a revelation is committed to writing, there is a greater possibility of transmitting it to those who speak and write in a different language. The message can be spread and copied with the assurance that the original thoughts will stay intact. Therefore, the message becomes accessible to more people.

6. THIS IS THE WAY THAT WE HUMANS COMMUNICATE

When human beings want to preserve a communication they put it in writing. Since God decided to communicate to human beings in words that we would understand, it makes sense that He would use the same method that we do to preserve our own communications—He put it in writing.

In fact, we read in the Scripture that the patriarch Job challenged God to put His words to Job into writing. We read the following.

> Why doesn't God All-Powerful listen and answer? If God has something against me, let him speak up or put it in writing! (Job 31:35 CEV).

God has answered Job's request. We have God's written revelation to us.

7. APART FROM A WRITTEN RECORD, THERE IS NO OTHER PRACTICAL WAY TO COMMUNICATE GOD'S TRUTH

As one thinks about the situation, there is really no other practical way in which God could have revealed Himself—except in written form. How else could He have imparted His infallible standard that would be available to every human being in every age?

8. WE HAVE A RESPONSIBILITY TO STUDY GOD'S REVELATION

Therefore, when all the information is considered, we find that a written revelation from God is absolutely essential. Because we have a written communication from the Lord, we have a responsibility to study it, and think about it. The psalmist wrote.

> How blessed is the one who does not follow the advice of the wicked, or stand in the pathway with sinners, or sit in the assembly of scoffers! Instead he finds pleasure in obeying the Lord's commands; he meditates on his commands day and night (Psalm 1:1-2 NET).

Joshua was told by the Lord to meditate on the Word of God. The Lord said to him.

> This book of the law shall not depart out of your mouth; you shall meditate on it day and night, so that you may be careful to act in accordance with all that is written in it. For then you shall make your way prosperous, and then you shall be successful (Joshua 1:8 NRSV).

We should do the same.

SUMMARY TO QUESTION 15
WHY DO WE NEED A WRITTEN REVELATION FROM GOD?

As we have just observed, it is essential that we have a written revelation from God—if we want to know who He is, and what He requires from us. An oral communication is beset with many problems—not the least of which is that the message would eventually be garbled. Furthermore, there would not be anyone to authoritatively tell us which version of the message was indeed the true "Word of God."

A written revelation solves this problem. Indeed, it provides a standard for all people for all time. It is timeless—an unchanging message. Consequently, it is crucial that God reveal Himself to the world in a written document—and this is precisely what He had done!

QUESTION 16

Is it Logical to Think That God Would Communicate to Humanity?

Some people have ruled out the possibility of God communicating with humanity. They believe a revelation from a divine being to humankind is not even possible. However, the idea that God would communicate to humanity and leave behind a written record makes sense for the following reasons.

1. IT IS CONSISTENT WITH WHAT WE KNOW ABOUT GOD FROM HIS CREATION: HE IS A GOD OF WISDOM AND PURPOSE

The God who created the universe reveals Himself to be a God of wisdom and purpose. Since everything in the observable universe has been created for a purpose this would certainly include His highest creation—humanity. If God created human beings for a purpose, it would be folly to assume that He would not reveal that purpose. Therefore, from what we know about God from His creation, it makes sense that He would give humanity some revelation of Himself.

2. GOD IS A PERSONAL GOD WHO HAS THE ABILITY TO COMMUNICATE

The Bible reveals that the God who exists is a personal God—that is, He has the characteristics of personhood. He thinks, feels, and can give and receive love. He also has the ability to communicate. The Bible says that God loves humanity. The most familiar verse in the Bible says.

> For God so loved the world that He gave His only begotten Son, that whoever believes in Him should not perish but have everlasting life (John 3:16 NKJV).

Since God loves His creation, the natural expectation is that He would reveal Himself to those whom He created.

3. IT IS NOT TOO DIFFICULT FOR HIM TO DO THIS

If God is all-powerful, He is certainly *able* to make Himself known to humanity. There is nothing lacking in His character that would stop Him from communicating. Jeremiah records the Lord saying.

> Behold, I *am* the LORD, the God of all flesh. Is there anything too hard for Me? (Jeremiah 32:27 NKJV).

The answer to this question is, "No." There is nothing too difficult for the Lord. He can do anything which is consistent with His holy character.

4. HE HAS MADE US WITH THE ABILITY TO COMMUNICATE WITH EACH OTHER

The Bible says that God made humanity in His image and His likeness. We read the following in the first chapter of the Book of Genesis.

> Then God said, "Let Us make man in Our image, according to Our likeness; let them have dominion over the fish of the sea, over the birds of the air, and over the cattle, over all the earth and over every creeping thing that creeps on the earth." So God created man in His own image; in the image of God He created him; male and female He created them. Then God blessed them, and God said to them, "Be fruitful and multiply; fill the earth and subdue it; have dominion over the fish of the sea, over the birds of the air, and over every living thing that moves on the earth" (Genesis 1:26-28 NKJV).

The New Living Translation translates these verses in this manner.

> Then God said, "Let us make people in our image, to be like
> ourselves. They will be masters over all life—the fish in the
> sea, the birds in the sky, and all the livestock, wild animals,
> and small animals." So God created people in his own image;
> God patterned them after himself; male and female he cre-
> ated them. God blessed them and told them, "Multiply and
> fill the earth and subdue it. Be masters over the fish and birds
> and all the animals" (Genesis 1:26-28 NLT).

Part of the image and likeness of God is the ability to give and receive
communication. Since both God and human beings have the ability
to communicate with others, it is perfectly logical to assume that God
would communicate with us.

5. WE HAVE A COMMUNICATION FROM GOD: THE BIBLE

With these factors considered, a final point to emphasize is that we do,
in fact, have a written communication that claims to be from God. That
communication, the Bible, shows us a God of love who has revealed
Himself to the human race. The prophet Isaiah emphasized this fact.

> Hear, O heavens, and give ear, O earth! For the LORD has
> spoken: "I have nourished and brought up children, and
> they have rebelled against Me; the ox knows its owner and
> the donkey its master's crib; but Israel does not know, My
> people do not consider" (Isaiah 1:2,3 NKJV).

The Bible says the Lord has indeed spoken.

Simon Peter recognized that Jesus had the words of eternal life. The
Bible says.

> Simon Peter answered him [Jesus], "Lord, to whom can we
> go? You have the words of eternal life" (John 6:68 NRSV).

Today, we find that the words of eternal life have come down to us from God's written communication to humanity—the Holy Scriptures. Without God's divine revelation in the Bible, we are left to our own ideas about who God is, and who we are.

In fact, any attempt to explain God is doomed to failure because each of us would merely project our own thoughts about who God is and then come up with the type of God we think should exist. There would be no consensus of opinion, and no basis of knowing whom, if anybody, was right in their opinions about God.

With God's divine revelation, as it is written in the Bible, there is no confusion surrounding God's character, or His purpose for humanity. We are fortunate that God has revealed His words to us so that we do not have any confusion.

So to sum up, humanity needs a divine revelation from God and God is able and willing to supply one. In fact, He has—the Bible. It is certainly reasonable to believe that a loving God would inform His creation about Himself, as well as about who we are, so that we do not have to stumble in the darkness. Indeed, His written Word lights our way!

SUMMARY TO QUESTION 16
IS IT LOGICAL TO THINK THAT GOD WOULD COMMUNICATE WITH HUMANITY?

It is logical to think that God would communicate with humanity. The very nature of God makes it reasonable that God would make Himself known to His creation. Since He created humankind for a purpose, it makes sense that He would reveal that purpose.

In addition, the God of the Bible is a personal God who loves those He has created. Consequently, we would expect Him to communicate to those whom He loves.

There is also the matter of God's power. Since God is all-powerful He is certainly able to communicate to His creation. God has also made humankind with the ability to give and receive communication. All of these truths make a divine revelation possible.

Therefore, a communication from God to humankind makes perfect sense and should logically be expected.

Finally, we have that communication—the Bible.

Is Human Language a Sufficient Means of Communication Between God and Humanity?

Is it possible for God to communicate to humanity in our own language? Is God too great to limit Himself to human words? Some have argued that an all-powerful God is too big to communicate with human beings. They assume that it is not even possible for this to happen.

The Bible, however, says that God has indeed communicated to us through the means of human language. Therefore, God is not too great to limit Himself to human language.

On the contrary, God is so great that He can communicate to human beings in human words. Human language, imperfect as it is, is sufficient for us understand some things about God.

A number of important points need to be made. They are as follows.

1. WE ARE LIKE GOD IN SOME WAYS: WE ARE MADE IN HIS IMAGE

First, the Bible says that we have been made in the image of God. In the Book of Genesis, we read about this.

> Then God said, "Let Us make man in Our image, according to Our likeness; let them have dominion over the fish of the sea, over the birds of the air, and over the cattle, over all the earth and over every creeping thing that creeps on the earth." So God created man in His own image; in the image of God

He created him; male and female He created them. Then God blessed them, and God said to them, "Be fruitful and multiply; fill the earth and subdue it; have dominion over the fish of the sea, over the birds of the air, and over every living thing that moves on the earth" (Genesis 1:26-28 NKJV).

Part of this image is the ability to give and receive communication. He has made us rational and intelligent beings. Humans have the ability to understand who God is—that is to the degree that He has revealed this to us.

2. HUMAN LANGUAGE IS FLAWED, BUT IT IS SUFFICIENT TO COMMUNICATE

God made human language to have a divinely ordained purpose—to communicate ideas, concepts, and personal feelings. Human language accomplishes these purposes successfully.

When Adam and Eve fell into sin everything about their character became marred. This includes human language. Human language, like everything else that is part of a human being, is touched by sin.

Despite this, God chose to use human language to reveal His divine truth. Although human beings are now in a sinful state, sin did not take away humanity's ability to understand God. God continued to reveal Himself to humanity after sin had entered our world.

After Adam sinned, we find that God called out to him. The Bible says.

But the Lord God called to the man and said to him, "Where are you?" And he said, "I heard the sound of you in the garden, and I was afraid, because I was naked, and I hid myself." He said, "Who told you that you were naked? Have you eaten of the tree of which I commanded you not to eat?" (Genesis 3:9-11 ESV).

Even after Adam sinned, he was still able to communicate with God. Human language is, therefore, a sufficient means for intelligent beings to communicate with one another.

The fact that we humans, do communicate with one another, makes this truth obvious. To argue otherwise would be nonsense. Humans can communicate with other humans across cultural and language barriers. All humans use their reasoning powers in basically the same way—no matter what their cultural background.

In addition, all humans have common experiences, and have the same basic needs. Human language, therefore, does accomplish the task for which it was originally created.

3. GOD USED THE LANGUAGE THAT WAS ALREADY AVAILABLE TO COMMUNICATE WITH HUMANITY

God reveals Himself to the extent that humans can receive it. From Scripture, we learn that God accommodated Himself to human language —He communicated to us in the words and concepts in which we can understand. In doing so, He used words that were already part of the spoken language at the time. As one studies the Bible, a person will discover the lack of new words and new definitions contained in Scripture. God used the words and definitions that people were familiar with to communicate His truth. While the truths were new, the words used to explain these truths were not new.

4. GOD AUDIBLY SPOKE TO HUMAN BEINGS IN A LANGUAGE THEY UNDERSTOOD

In addition, we find that God Himself has actually spoken in an audible voice to human beings by means of human language. Scripture is filled with examples of God actually speaking to people in the language which they normally spoke. We also find that the people, though sinful, clearly understood what God had said to them.

For example, the risen Christ appeared to Saul of Tarsus on the Damascus road. The Bible records it as follows.

> And falling to the ground he heard a voice saying to him, "Saul, Saul, why are you persecuting me?" And he said, "Who are you, Lord?" And he said, "I am Jesus, whom you are persecuting. But rise and enter the city, and you will be told what you are to do" (Acts 9:4-6 ESV).

Saul obviously understood the message that came from the Lord—there was no language problem.

5. THE WORD OF GOD WAS WRITTEN IN HUMAN LANGUAGE

The words of Scripture are also God's Words. Although human beings, in human language, wrote down the words of Scripture, these words are still considered to be the Word of God. The written Scriptures are God's communication with humanity.

Furthermore, the words that God spoke to people and are recorded in Scripture were spoken in understandable, human language. Although they originated with God, they were communicated so that humans could understand. The fact that God spoke human words does not limit the divine authority of the message.

6. HIS WORD IS EXPECTED TO BE OBEYED

Moreover, God held the people responsible for obeying His communication. The words that the prophets spoke to the people were just as authoritative as if God has personally spoken them. Disobeying the prophets was the same as disobeying the Lord. The Lord said to Moses.

> I will raise up for them a prophet like you from among their brothers. I will put My words in his mouth, and he will tell them everything I command him. I will hold accountable whoever does not listen to My words that he speaks in My

name. But the prophet who dares to speak a message in My name that I have not commanded him to speak, or who speaks in the name of other gods—that prophet must die (Deuteronomy 18:18-20 HCSB).

The New Living Translation translates these verses as follows.

I will raise up a prophet like you from among their fellow Israelites. I will tell that prophet what to say, and he will tell the people everything I command him. I will personally deal with anyone who will not listen to the messages the prophet proclaims on my behalf. But any prophet who claims to give a message from another god or who falsely claims to speak for me must die (Deuteronomy 18:18-20 NLT).

The fact that God expected obedience from His people shows that His words, as spoken through His prophets, could easily be understood.

7. GOD BECAME A HUMAN BEING TO PERSONALLY COMMUNICATE WITH US

Finally, we have the fact of Jesus Christ—the eternal God became a human being. When God did become a man, He spoke human words The Bible says.

And the Word was made flesh, and dwelt among us (John 1:14 KJV).

The purpose was to show us what God is like. John also wrote.

No one has ever seen God. The only one, himself God, who is in closest fellowship with the Father, has made God known (John 1:18 NRSV).

God became a man and personally spoke to humanity in human words so that we can know what He is like. This is another indication that human language has the ability to communicate God's truth. Therefore, when all the evidence is in, we can conclude that human language is indeed a sufficient means of God communicating His truths to humanity.

SUMMARY TO QUESTION 17
IS HUMAN LANGUAGE A SUFFICIENT MEANS OF COMMUNICATION FROM GOD TO HUMANITY?

God has established points of contact between Himself and the human race. Indeed, God created human language so that He could communicate unchanging truths about Himself.

In fact, there is nothing inherently impossible, or unreasonable, that the living God would communicate with His creation through human language. Since human beings of all nations are able to communicate with each other through language, then it certainly is not impossible for God to do so. While language is not a perfect means of communication, it is a sufficient means.

The Bible itself shows that God gave His revelation of Himself in words and concepts that human beings can and do understand. When the risen Christ communicated to Saul of Tarsus from heaven, Saul understood and obeyed. In fact, the Bible expects humans to understand God's communication. This shows that it is clear that human language is a sufficient means for God to communicate with humanity.

Finally, the Bible says that God became a human being in the Person of Jesus Christ—to let us know what He is like and what He requires from us. When Christ came He spoke in human words. This is another indication of the sufficiency of human language.

To Whom Was the Bible Written?

Whom did God intend to read the words of Scripture? Was it everyone, or was it only meant to be read by an elite few? Who is meant to read the Bible?

A number of important points need to be made about this issue. They are as follows.

1. SCRIPTURE IS WRITTEN TO EVERYONE

The appeal of the Bible is universal—addressed to all humanity. It is a book that everyone can understand. The Bible says the following happened when Jesus spoke,

> And the great throng heard him gladly (Mark 12:37 ESV).

The multitudes listened and followed Him. They understood exactly what He said.

Jesus encouraged the children to be brought to Him—for they could understand His message. We read the following in Matthew's gospel.

> But Jesus said, "Let the little children come to me and do not hinder them, for to such belongs the kingdom of heaven" (Matthew 19:14 ESV).

ALL SCRIPTURE IS BENEFICIAL

While certain parts of the Scripture are written to individuals, and other parts to specific groups, even these have both special and universal application. In fact, the Bible testifies that all Scripture is beneficial. Paul wrote.

> All Scripture is breathed out by God and profitable for teaching, for reproof, for correction, and for training in righteousness, that the man of God may be competent, equipped for every good work (2 Timothy 3:16,17 ESV).

The New Living Translation says.

> All Scripture is inspired by God and is useful to teach us what is true and to make us realize what is wrong in our lives. It straightens us out and teaches us to do what is right. It is God's way of preparing us in every way, fully equipped for every good thing God wants us to do (2 Timothy 3:16,17 NLT).

The Bible has something to say to everyone.

2. THE BIBLE IS WRITTEN IN EVERYDAY LANGUAGE

One way that we know the Bible was written for everyone is the language in which it was composed. As recently as about one hundred years ago, we did not possess any Greek writings that were contemporary with the New Testament. The Greek of the New Testament was different from the classical Greek of Plato and Sophocles. Most scholars speculated that it was some special kind of "Holy Ghost" language—not the ordinary speech of that day.

This all changed at the end of the nineteenth century. In a garbage dump in Egypt, the discovery was made of the letters, contracts, receipts, etc. of ordinary people who lived at the same time as Jesus. It became clear from these writings that the New Testament was written in the same common, everyday language of the people—not some special Bible language. This reinforces the idea that the Bible was written to the masses, not just to an elite few.

3. THE BIBLE IS AN UNDERSTANDABLE BOOK

The Bible has been written in such a way that everyone can understand it. This, of course, does not mean that everyone will understand it, or that any one person will understand everything in it. Neither does it mean that a person will understand it the first time they read it. The more one reads, and studies the Bible, the more it will be understood.

The Apostle Paul compared his speaking to the church at Thessalonica as a mother caring and feeding her own children. He wrote.

> As apostles of Christ we certainly had a right to make some demands of you, but we were as gentle among you as a mother feeding and caring for her own children (1 Thessalonians 2:7 NLT).

He spoke in plain language that they could understand. In fact, He spoke in the same way that a mother speaks of her children. As the mother speaks to her children in language they can understand, God's Word speaks to us in language we can understand.

4. EVERYONE IS HELD RESPONSIBLE TO OBEY ITS TEACHINGS

Scripture assumes its message is clear because everyone is held responsible to respond to it. The Bible claims to have universal authority over all people everywhere.

In fact, there are only two categories of people according to the Bible—believers and unbelievers. The New Testament says.

> He who believes in the Son has everlasting life; and he who does not believe the Son shall not see life, but the wrath of God abides on him (John 3:36 NKJV).

The New Living Translation reads

> And all who believe in God's Son have eternal life. Those who don't obey the Son will never experience eternal life, but the wrath of God remains upon them (John 3:36 NLT).

The fact that the Bible separates humanity into these two categories is another indication that all people are held responsible to believe its message. Therefore, it is necessary for everyone to know the contents of Scripture—for they alone contain the words of life.

SUMMARY TO QUESTION 18
TO WHOM WAS THE BIBLE WRITTEN?

The evidence demonstrates that the Bible was written to every human being, not to just a select few. We now understand the language of the New Testament was the common written and spoken language of the time.

The Bible was not written in some special holy language to meet the needs of a few. Scripture has been composed in such a way as to be understandable to the masses.

Furthermore, God will hold everyone responsible as to how they receive His Word. This is another indication that the Bible was written with everyone in mind. Therefore, every person needs to pay close attention to its message.

Are There Other Written Sources of Religious Truth From God Apart From the Bible?

No. While there are many other religious writings that claim to reveal "ultimate truth," the Bible clearly says that it is the sole written source of our knowledge about the one true living God. It is the only written revelation that He has given humanity. The following points need to be considered.

1. THE BIBLE COMMANDS NOT TO ADD OR SUBTRACT FROM GOD'S REVEALED WORD

There are warnings contained in Scripture not to add or subtract from what God has revealed. Moses wrote.

> You shall not add to the word which I command you, nor take from it, that you may keep the commandments of the LORD your God which I command you (Deuteronomy 4:2 NKJV).

In the Book of Proverbs, we read something similar. It says.

> Every word of God is flawless; he is a shield to those who take refuge in him. Do not add to his words, or he will rebuke you and prove you a liar (Proverbs 30:5,6 NIV).

The Book of Revelation closes by giving this warning.

I warn everyone who hears the words of the prophecy of this book: If anyone of you adds anything to them, God will add to you the plagues described in this scroll. And if anyone of you takes words away from this scroll of prophecy, God will take away from you your share in the tree of life and in the holy city, which are described in this scroll (Revelation 22:18,19 NIV).

God's Words are important to Him—no human being should add or subtract from them. Since He is the only God that exists, His words alone are the final standard of right and wrong.

2. ALL OTHER WAYS TO GOD ARE FALSE

The Bible warns its readers of false prophets and false teachings. John wrote to the readers of his day about such. He said.

Dear friends, do not believe every spirit, but test the spirits to determine if they are from God, because many false prophets have gone out into the world (1 John 4:1 HCSB).

Jesus warned of those who offer other ways to approach God apart from Him. We read the following in the gospel of John.

Those who heard Jesus use this illustration didn't understand what he meant, so he explained it to them. "I assure you, I am the gate for the sheep," he said. "All others who came before me were thieves and robbers. But the true sheep did not listen to them. Yes, I am the gate. Those who come in through me will be saved. Wherever they go, they will find green pastures. The thief's purpose is to steal and kill and destroy. My purpose is to give life in all its fullness" (John 10:6-10 NLT).

The Apostle Paul warned about false teachers who claimed to speak for Christ. He wrote the following to the church at Galatia.

I am astonished that you are so quickly deserting the one who called you in the grace of Christ and are turning to a different gospel—not that there is another gospel, but there are some who are confusing you and want to pervert the gospel of Christ. But even if we or an angel from heaven should proclaim to you a gospel contrary to what we proclaimed to you, let that one be accursed! As we have said before, so now I repeat, if anyone proclaims to you a gospel contrary to what you received, let that one be accursed (Galatians 1:6-9 NRSV).

Only the gospel, or the good news, that has been revealed in the New Testament is the true gospel—all other so-called gospels are false.

The Bible says that there are also false apostles who preach a different Jesus. These types of people were around in Paul's day. He warned the Corinthians about them. He wrote.

I hope you will be patient with me as I keep on talking like a fool. Please bear with me. I am jealous for you with the jealousy of God himself. For I promised you as a pure bride to one husband, Christ. But I fear that somehow you will be led away from your pure and simple devotion to Christ, just as Eve was deceived by the serpent. You seem to believe whatever anyone tells you, even if they preach about a different Jesus than the one we preach, or a different Spirit than the one you received, or a different kind of gospel than the one you believed. . . These people are counterfeit apostles, dishonest workers disguising themselves as apostles of Christ. There is nothing astonishing in this; even Satan disguises himself as an angel of light (2 Corinthians 11:1-4, 13-14 NLT).

The Corinthians seemed to believe the message brought by these false teachers. Paul rebuked them for this. That is why it is essential that we know and understand the content of the genuine message that the Lord has given to humanity.

3. THE FAITH HAS BEEN DELIVERED ONCE AND FOR ALL DELIVERED TO HUMANITY

There is something more. The Bible says that the faith has been once-and-for-all delivered to believers. Jude wrote about this. He said.

> Dear friends, although I was eager to write you about the salvation we share, I found it necessary to write and exhort you to contend for the faith that was delivered to the saints once for all (Jude 3 HCSB).

The faith has been delivered in the Scriptures and nowhere else. It is the only source of authority to which one can go to discover God's truth.

CONCLUSION: THE BIBLE ALONE IS THE ONLY INFALLIBLE SOURCE OF TRUTH ABOUT GOD

Consequently, the Bible is the only written revelation that God has given to the human race. There is only one God who exists, and He has chosen to reveal Himself through only one written source— the Scriptures. No other source of divine truth should be consulted because no other source is divine. The Bible alone is the one guide for all humanity.

SUMMARY TO QUESTION 19
ARE THERE OTHER WRITTEN SOURCES OF RELIGIOUS TRUTH FROM GOD APART FROM THE BIBLE?

It is clear that the Bible does not present itself as one of several options for religious truth. It claims to be God's authoritative Word. The Bible consistently maintains that any work, religious or otherwise, which teaches anything to the contrary is, at that point, wrong. As far as the Bible is concerned, it is all or nothing.

If we accept it, we must accept it as ultimately authoritative. It must be the standard by which we judge all other writings that attempt to convey spiritual truth.

If God Was Behind the Writing of a Book, Then What Should We Expect From It?

There are certain things that a person would expect from any book that was divinely inspired, or overseen, by God. They include, at least, the following six things.

1. IT WOULD HAVE UNIVERSAL APPEAL

Any book from the living God would have a universal appeal. Everyone, in every place, would be touched by its message. It would not be limited to any one culture, or any one time in history. It would be for all people for all times.

2. IT WOULD BE UNDERSTANDABLE BY THE MASSES

Since God is perfect, He would be the perfect communicator. Therefore, any book that had God's authority behind it would have to be understandable to the masses. God would choose writers that would communicate in such a way that all peoples would be able to understand. It would not matter what language they spoke, or what culture they came from.

3. IT WOULD BE TRUE IN ALL THAT IT SAYS

Any book that God was behind its writing would be assumed to be true in all that it said. If God is true, then His Word must also be true—for the words of a person reflects their character.

Thus, there would be no lies or false promises in a book from God. Everything that is said or taught could be trusted.

4. IT WOULD BE THE MOST PROFOUND BOOK EVER WRITTEN

The truths found in a book that would come from God would make it the most profound book ever written. In its pages, we would expect to find truths that were found nowhere else. Even the wisest of us could not expect to completely understand the depths of its teachings. Indeed, we would be surprised if everything about God could be easily understood.

5. IT WOULD BE THE MOST INFLUENTIAL BOOK EVER WRITTEN

We would also expect a book that God divinely inspired to be the most influential book that has ever been written. We would assume that it would have an impact like no other book in history. Nothing could stop its impact if God was behind it.

6. IT WOULD BE THE MOST IMPORTANT BOOK EVER WRITTEN

Finally, any book that came from God would be the most important book ever written. It would hold the secrets to such questions as: Who is God? Who are human beings? Why do we exist?

No other book would even come close in rivaling it in importance.

THESE EXPECTATIONS ARE MET BY SCRIPTURE

Scripture meets and exceeds all these expectations. We can make the following observations about the Bible.

1. THE BIBLE DOES HAVE UNIVERSAL APPEAL

The Bible, from the start, has had a universal appeal. Although the main events come from the Ancient Near East, the truths of the Bible have molded Western civilization.

In every country in which it goes, the impact of the Bible changes lives. The truths of the Bible are just as relevant for those living in China as they are for those living in Africa. Wherever we go into the world, we find the truths of the Bible appealing to the human heart. Young and old, rich and poor, the intelligent and the simple, the Bible is for everyone.

2. THE BIBLE IS UNDERSTANDABLE TO THE MASSES

The Bible has been written in a style that is easy to understand. Even little children can read its stories with understanding. God uses our human words, wording, and meaning to clearly communicate His truth to everyone. The Bible is indeed a book for all people.

3. SCRIPTURE CLAIMS TO BE TRUE IN ALL THAT IT RECORDS

The Bible itself claims to be the true Word of God. Over five thousand times in the Bible we have phrases such as, "God said," or the "Lord said." It claims to accurately record truths about God. Add to this, all the evidence that we now possess, whether it be historical or scientific, indicates Scripture is true in all that it says. If the Bible is true, then we should submit to the commands it gives.

4. THE BIBLE CONTAINS PROFOUND TEACHINGS

Despite being written in a style that is easy to understand, no one, even after a lifetime of study, can fully understand all its truths. No matter how much a person knows about the Bible, they can always learn more. Paul wrote.

> Oh, the depth of the riches of the wisdom and knowledge of God! How unsearchable his judgments, and his paths beyond tracing out! (Romans 11:33 NIV).

Isaiah the prophet recorded God revealing the differences between His thoughts and ours. The Lord said the following.

> For my thoughts are not your thoughts, neither are your ways
> my ways, saith the LORD. For as the heavens are higher than
> the earth, so are my ways higher than your ways, and my
> thoughts than your thoughts (Isaiah 55:8,9 KJV).

The truths of Scripture are profound indeed.

5. THE BIBLE IS MOST INFLUENTIAL BOOK EVERY WRITTEN

In our world, no book has had near the influence as the Bible has had.
It is easily the most influential book that has ever been written. The
effects of the Bible in the lives of human beings, as well as in human
history, testify to its divine authority. Although it is one of the oldest
books ever written, it is still the best-selling book in the world. No
book has been so often translated, quoted, attacked, and loved as the
Bible. The Bible has been printed more times, it has been more often
translated, and it is the most widely read of any book in history. No
other book even comes close.

Furthermore, the Bible has promoted literacy in the world. For example, there are many languages that have been now reduced to writing
for the very first time. This has occurred so that the books of the Bible
might be translated into these languages and then placed into some
written form.

The Bible is different from all other books in its effect on individual
human beings and on the history of nations of the world. It is not only
the all-time best seller, it still appeals to both the hearts and minds of
all people in every nation. Wherever the message of Scripture has gone,
it has been embraced by every race, nation, or tribe.

This is true whether the people are rich or poor, young or old, scholars
or laymen, kings or commoners. People of literally every background
and walk of life receive the message of Scripture with gladness. There
is no other book that has ever had such universal appeal, nor has any
other book produced such lasting effects as has the Bible

6. THE BIBLE IS THE MOST IMPORTANT BOOK EVER WRITTEN

If God was personally behind the writing of a book, we would expect it to be the most important book that has ever been written. Since it would tell us who God is, who we are, why we are here, and what our destiny is, no book would rival its importance. The Bible is that Book! It is the most important Book that has ever been written. Therefore, the Bible should be studied more than any other book.

All things considered, the Bible is just the sort of book we should expect as coming from God. Indeed, it has the credentials that we would imagine.

SUMMARY TO QUESTION 20
IF GOD WAS BEHIND THE WRITING OF A BOOK, THEN WHAT SHOULD WE EXPECT FROM IT?

There are a number of things that would be expected if God was to be behind the writing of a book. This book would have to address the basic needs of humanity.

We would expect it to have universal appeal—it should be relevant to every person no matter when they lived in history. This book should also be understood by the masses—not just an elite few.

This book should be true in all that it says—if it comes from a wise and perfect God.

In addition, we would expect it to be the most profound book that has ever been written—its truths could never be fully appreciated.

We would also expect it to be the most influential book ever written.

Finally, it would be the most important book ever written.

The Bible meets all these expectations. If any book could make a claim to be God's Word, then it would be the Bible.

What Power Does the Bible Have to Change Lives?

One of the unique things about the Bible is the power of its message to change lives. Like no other book ever written, the message of Scripture has the ability to transform lives. We read about the power of God's Word in both testaments. The psalmist wrote.

> The instructions of the Lord are perfect, reviving the soul. The decrees of the Lord are trustworthy, making wise the simple. The commandments of the Lord are right, bringing joy to the heart. The commands of the Lord are clear, giving insight for living (Psalm 19:7-8 NLT).

According to this passage, the Word of God is perfect, trustworthy, right, brings joy to the heart, clear, and give us insight for living. It has the ability to change someone's life.

A number of important observations need to be made.

1. THE MESSAGE OF THE BIBLE IS LIVING AND POWERFUL

The writer to the Hebrews declared the Word of God to be living and powerful. He wrote the following.

> Indeed, the word of God is living and active, sharper than any two-edged sword, piercing until it divides soul from

spirit, joints from marrow; it is able to judge the thoughts and intentions of the heart (Hebrews 4:12 NRSV).

The words of Scripture, which are the words of God, can do what no other book can do.

2. THE BIBLICAL MESSAGE HAS POWER OVER UNBELIEVERS

Scripture has power over both believers and unbelievers. Paul told Timothy the Scriptures are able make unbelievers wise unto salvation.

> But as for you, continue in what you have learned and have become convinced of, because you know those from whom you learned it, and how from infancy you have known the Holy Scriptures, which are able to make you wise for salvation through faith in Christ Jesus (2 Timothy 3:14,15 NIV).

From Holy Scripture alone, unbelievers discover how to have a personal relationship with the living God through Jesus Christ.

3. SCRIPTURE HAS POWER OVER BELIEVERS TO CHANGE THEIR LIVES

Scripture also has a profound effect on those who believe in God's promises. Isaiah the prophet records the Lord saying.

> As the rain and the snow come down from heaven, and do not return to it without watering the earth and making it bud and flourish, so that it yields seed for the sower and bread for the eater, so is my word that goes out from my mouth: It will not return to me empty, but will accomplish what I desire and achieve the purpose for which I sent it (Isaiah 55:10,11 NIV).

The words of Scripture have the ability to transform the lives of those who believe in its truths, and obey its commands.

4. THE MESSAGE OF THE BIBLE CAN BE READ WITH PROFIT OVER AND OVER AGAIN

One of the things that separates the Bible from any other book that has ever been written is that its message can be read over and over again without exhausting the contents. No other book in the world can make such a claim. Millions have testified to the unsearchable riches that are contained in the pages of Scripture.

No matter how many times a person reads the Bible, there is always something new that can be learned. Why is this so? What makes the Bible so special? The answer is simple. It is God's Book to humanity, and it contains His unsearchable riches.

SUMMARY TO QUESTION 21
WHAT POWER DOES THE BIBLE HAVE TO CHANGE LIVES?

The Bible is unique among books in that it has the power to change lives. It reveals to the unbeliever the way of eternal salvation. To the believer, it is life changing in its truth. Indeed, the Scripture can be read time and time again with new things learned upon each reading.

No other book has such ability. This is another indication that the Bible is what it claims to be—the Word of God.

What Is the Clarity of Scripture? (Perspicuity)

The clarity of Scripture is also known as "perspicuity." Basically this means that the message of the Scriptures can be understood by the great masses of people who wish to understand it. God's Word has been revealed in such a way that everyone who wants to know what it means can make sense of what it says. In addition, they are able to live in accordance with these truths.

THIS IS THE TEACHING OF SCRIPTURE – THE MESSAGE IS CLEAR

The idea of the clarity of Scripture is something that the Bible often teaches about itself. We find this taught in the Old Testament, the teachings of Jesus, and the New Testament letters. We can make the following observations.

1. THE OLD TESTAMENT ASSUMES GOD'S WORD IS CLEAR

Moses told the people of the nation of Israel that the commands of the Lord were to be studied by all. He wrote.

> These commandments that I give you today are to be upon your hearts. Impress them on your children. Talk about them when you sit at home and when you walk along the road, when you lie down and when you get up (Deuteronomy 6:6,7 NIV).

Notice that Moses not only expected the adults to understand what he had written, he also expected their children to understand it. This emphasizes the fact that the truths can easily be understood.

The Contemporary English Version puts it this way.

> Memorize his laws and tell them to your children over and over again. Talk about them all the time, whether you're at home or walking along the road or going to bed at night, or getting up in the morning (Deuteronomy 6:6,7 CEV).

The Bible also says that the simple become wise through reading and applying God's Word. The psalmist wrote.

> The law of the LORD is perfect, reviving the soul. The statutes of the LORD are trustworthy, making wise the simple (Psalm 19:7 NIV).

The psalmist also wrote.

> The unfolding of your words gives light; it imparts understanding to the simple (Psalm 119:130 ESV).

Therefore, the Old Testament teaches that the commandments of God can be understood by everyone—not just an elite few.

2. JESUS TESTIFIED TO THE CLARITY OF SCRIPTURE

We discover the same emphasis in the New Testament. In fact, we find Jesus often answering a question with the question, "Have you not read?" The idea is that the Scriptures have the answer to their question, if they would only read what it said. In a dialogue with the religious leaders, He said.

> But now, as to whether there will be a resurrection of the dead—haven't you ever read about this in the Scriptures? Long after Abraham, Isaac, and Jacob had died, God said,

'I am the God of Abraham, the God of Isaac, and the God of Jacob.' So he is the God of the living, not the dead (Matthew 22:31,32 NET).

On the other hand, we never find Jesus saying the Scriptures were unclear about any subject. To the contrary, He always assumed the problem was failure to accept what the Scripture clearly said.

On the same occasion, Jesus said to the religious leaders.

> You are mistaken, not knowing the Scriptures nor the power of God (Matthew 22:29 NKJV).

Whether speaking to the multitudes, His own disciples, or the religious authorities, Jesus assumed that all of them could understand the Scripture.

3. THE NEW TESTAMENT WRITINGS WERE EXPECTED TO BE READ OUT LOUD TO CHURCHES

The New Testament letters that have become part of Scripture were, for the most part, written to congregations. Many of the people were Gentiles, non-Jews, with little or no background in the Old Testament Scripture. Yet there was the assumption that they could understand the things that were written to them.

The letters Paul wrote were to be read out loud to the various churches to which they were addressed. To the Colossians he wrote.

> Give my greetings to the brothers in Laodicea, and to Nympha and the church in her home. When this letter has been read among you, have it read also in the church of the Laodiceans; and see that you also read the letter from Laodicea (Colossians 4:15,16 HCSB).

This assumes everyone, including the children, would be able to understand what he had written to them.

Paul also wrote the following to the Corinthians.

> My letters have been straightforward, and there is nothing written between the lines and nothing you can't understand. I hope someday you will fully understand us, even if you don't fully understand us now. Then on the day when our Lord Jesus comes back again, you will be proud of us in the same way we are proud of you (2 Corinthians 1:13-14 NLT).

Paul assumes that his readers can understand what he wrote. However, he also said that the people must listen carefully to make certain their understanding is not merely partial. Paul expressed confidence that they are able to do this.

Therefore, from the totality of Scripture, we find that the Bible is assumed to be understandable. Indeed, to assert that God would offer humanity a revelation of Himself that could not be understood does not make any sense. Why would He take the time to have the books composed, copied, and preserved if they could not be understood in a straightforward manner?

4. WE STILL NEED THE HELP OF THE HOLY SPIRIT IN UNDERSTANDING THESE TRUTHS

There is also a spiritual dimension in the understanding of Scripture. We need God's help in understanding the truths of Scripture. Paul wrote about this. He said.

> The natural person does not accept the things of the Spirit of God, for they are folly to him, and he is not able to understand them because they are spiritually discerned (1 Corinthians 2:14 ESV).

While the Bible is written in such a way that it can be clearly understood, those who are not willing to accept its truth will not appreciate the full import of what it says.

Jesus said that people could know whether or not His teaching came from God. We read the following in the Gospel of John.

> If anyone's will is to do God's will, he will know whether the teaching is from God or whether I am speaking on my own authority (John 7:17 ESV).

Jesus said that He spoke in stories, or parables, so that those who wanted to know the truth could know it. He said.

> That is why I tell these stories, because people see what I do, but they don't really see. They hear what I say, but they don't really hear, and they don't understand. This fulfills the prophecy of Isaiah, which says: 'You will hear my words, but you will not understand; you will see what I do, but you will not perceive its meaning. For the hearts of these people are hardened, and their ears cannot hear, and they have closed their eyes—so their eyes cannot see, and their ears cannot hear, and their hearts cannot understand, and they cannot turn to me and let me heal them.' But blessed are your eyes, because they see; and your ears, because they hear. I assure you, many prophets and godly people have longed to see and hear what you have seen and heard, but they could not (Matthew 13:13-17 NLT).

Jesus taught in such a way that those who want to hear His truth can clearly understand it. On the other hand, those who have closed their eyes and ears to God's truth will not understand it. Scripture will seem like nonsense to them.

Therefore, to correctly understand God's message in Scripture, we must be willing to be taught. Indeed, we must ask the Lord to open our spiritual eyes to His truth.

SUMMARY TO QUESTION 22
WHAT IS THE CLARITY OF SCRIPTURE? (PERSPICUITY)

God has made His message understandable to humanity. The clarity of Scripture is also known as perspicuity. This means that the basic message of Scripture has been clearly revealed so that everyone can understand it. The Bible is a book to be understood by the masses—it does not contain secret or hidden messages from God.

We find the clarity of Scripture taught in the Old Testament, the teachings of Jesus, and the New Testament letters. Therefore, no one has any excuse.

However, there is a spiritual dimension to God's truth that only believers will understand. This can only be done through the help of the Holy Spirit.

Because the Scripture Is Clear Does This Mean Everything Can Be Easily Understood?

The doctrine of the clarity of Scripture does teach that the message of the Bible can be clearly understood. However, it does not mean that all parts of the Bible are easily understood. Indeed, some parts are not easy to understand. From Scripture, we discover the following facts.

1. PETER SAID PAUL'S WRITINGS WERE HARD TO UNDERSTAND

Peter acknowledged that some things in Scripture were difficult to understand. He said the following about some of the things the Apostle Paul taught.

> Don't forget that the Lord is patient because he wants people to be saved. This is also what our dear friend Paul said when he wrote you with the wisdom that God had given him. Paul talks about these same things in all his letters, but part of what he says is hard to understand. Some ignorant and unsteady people even destroy themselves by twisting what he said. They do the same thing with other Scriptures too (2 Peter 3:15,16 CEV).

Peter realized some of Paul's wisdom was difficult to understand. However, even in Peter's statement we find that Paul's writings were understandable. Peter said that Paul's words were difficult to understand, but they were not impossible to understand. Also it was only some of the things that Paul wrote that were difficult to understand—it was not all of the things.

2. THERE ARE MORE PARTS THAT ARE CLEAR THAN ARE PROBLEMATIC

The good news is there is much more in Scripture that is clear than is problematic. While there are areas of difficulty, these parts are small in comparison to the totality of Scripture. Most of the Scripture is absolutely clear. Therefore, we do not have to hand the problems over to experts. This is because of the remarkable agreement among believers on the basic teachings of the faith.

3. THERE IS A ROLE FOR TEACHERS AND SCHOLARS TO INSTRUCT BELIEVERS

There are, however, problem areas in Scripture. This is where the role of teachers and Bible scholars comes into play. God has given the church people who are able to diligently study the Scripture. They are then able to explain their findings to others. Paul wrote about them in the following manner.

> And He personally gave some to be apostles, some prophets, some evangelists, some pastors and teachers, for the training of the saints in the work of ministry, to build up the body of Christ, until we all reach unity in the faith and in the knowledge of God's Son, growing into a mature man with a stature measured by Christ's fullness (Ephesians 4:11-13 HCSB).

From this passage, we find that God has given the church people with special gifts. Therefore, we should take advantage of the teaching gifts that God has given to His people. Teachers have been given to the church by God, and we need to take advantage of their gifts.

For one thing, scholars are able to help correct false teachers. Paul wrote to Titus about the qualifications of an elder.

He must have a strong and steadfast belief in the trustworthy message he was taught; then he will be able to encourage others with right teaching and show those who oppose it where they are wrong (Titus 1:9 NLT)

To Timothy, he wrote.

They should gently teach those who oppose the truth. Perhaps God will change those people's hearts, and they will believe the truth (2 Timothy 2:25 NLT).

They are able to answer new questions that arise as well as refine and state the truth more precisely.

While God has given scholars to the church, these scholars do not speak for the church. They have no right to decide what we believe. Bible scholars do not consist of some governing elite group. Therefore, we should not assume that scholars always get things right—or always get things wrong for that matter! Every Bible teacher recognizes his or her own limitations.

4. WE SHOULD APPRECIATE AND TAKE ADVANTAGE OF HERITAGE OF TEACHERS AND BIBLE SCHOLARS

We also have a heritage of two thousand years of godly people interpreting Scripture. We should not ignore this resource. It is important that we find out what others have said in the past, as well as the ongoing work of biblical scholars. We should learn from the work of others. They have much to teach us.

5. THE HOLY SPIRIT HAS A TEACHING MINISTRY TO ALL BELIEVERS

There is also the teaching ministry of the Holy Spirit that must be considered. The Bible promises that the Holy Spirit will teach believers. Jesus said.

> When the Advocate comes, whom I will send you from the
> Father—the Spirit of truth who goes out from the Father—he
> will testify about me. . . I have many more things to say to
> you, but you cannot bear them now. But when he, the Spirit
> of truth, comes, he will guide you into all truth. For he will
> not speak on his own authority, but will speak whatever he
> hears, and will tell you what is to come (John 15:26; 16:12-12
> NET).

He is the ultimate teacher for believers. He is the One who takes the
teachings of Scripture and makes them real to us.

6. THERE IS NO GUARANTEE THAT WE WILL UNDERSTAND EVERYTHING

While the Holy Spirit does indeed teach all believers, we must be careful not to make hasty conclusions regarding His ministry. Believing in
the teaching ministry of the Holy Spirit does not guarantee that we
will instantly understand everything. For a person to know what the
Scripture says and means, involves both study and thought. This is why
the Bible commands us to study God's Word. Paul wrote.

> Do your best to present yourself to God as one approved, a
> worker who has no need to be ashamed, rightly handling the
> word of truth (2 Timothy 2:15 ESV).

The Contemporary English Version translates this verse as follows.

> Do your best to win God's approval as a worker who doesn't
> need to be ashamed and who teaches only the true message
> (2 Timothy 2:15 CEV).

Studying the Scripture takes work. Time and effort must be expended
if we are to know what God's Word says. However, the results are well
worth the effort.

SUMMARY TO QUESTION 23
BECAUSE THE SCRIPTURE IS CLEAR DOES THIS MEAN EVERYTHING CAN BE EASILY UNDERSTOOD?

The idea that the Scriptures are clear does not mean that every passage will be easy to understand. The Bible itself testifies that some parts are difficult to understand. Peter acknowledged this about Paul's writings. Yet these parts were not impossible to understand.

The Bible also promises that the Holy Spirit will teach believers. This, however, is not a guarantee that we will immediately understand everything written within its pages. Understanding Scripture takes study and work.

The Bible says that God has given to the church certain people who are able to teach His truth. We also have a heritage of two thousand years of people attempting to understand difficulties in Scripture. Consequently, we should take advantage of those gifts that God has given certain individuals—as well as the knowledge that we can learn from the past.

What Is the Sufficiency of Scripture?

One of the most important doctrines with respect to the Bible is known as the "sufficiency of Scripture." The sufficiency of Scripture can be simply defined as follows: In the Bible alone, God has given humanity all things that are necessary for the proper understanding of who He is, who we are, how He has acted in the past, and what He expects from us.

The basic idea behind the sufficiency of Scripture is that nothing else needs to be revealed to humanity about God, or His plan for the human race. The Bible is the record of all of the things that God thought humanity needed to know about Him. In other words, the Scriptures are complete and sufficient for belief and behavior. Nothing needs to be added to them!

The following points need to be made about the sufficiency of Scripture.

1. THE BIBLE ALONE HAS THE ANSWERS TO LIFE'S MOST IMPORTANT QUESTIONS

The Bible contains the things, which God thought that we humans should know, on a number of different topics. His teaching on any subject is sufficient for us. In other words, we do not have to go elsewhere to find answers. The Bible says the faith has been once-and-for-all entrusted to believers. Jude wrote.

> Dear friends, although I have been eager to write to you about our common salvation, I now feel compelled instead to write to encourage you to contend earnestly for the faith that was once for all entrusted to the saints (Jude 3 NET).

Consequently, people are able to search the Bible for themselves and find out the important truths about God in its pages. His Word is enough.

For example, the Bible alone holds the key to salvation from sin. The Apostle Paul wrote to Timothy.

> And how from childhood you have been acquainted with the sacred writings, which are able to make you wise for salvation through faith in Christ Jesus (2 Timothy 3:15 ESV).

Paul emphasizes that it is from the Bible alone that we learn that forgiveness of sins must come through Jesus Christ. We do not have to look elsewhere for answers concerning how we are to be saved from sin.

James confirmed that God used the words found in Scripture to bring the message of salvation or the "new birth." He wrote.

> He wanted us to be his own special people, and so he sent the true message to give us new birth (James 1:18 CEV).

Therefore, the Holy Scripture provides us everything that we need to know about the central questions of life. It alone is where we go to find the answers.

2. EVERYTHING THAT WE NEED TO KNOW ABOUT GOD HAS BEEN REVEALED TO US: NOT EVERYTHING WE MAY WANT TO KNOW

While the Scriptures contain everything humanity needs to know about God, it does not reveal everything that we may desire to know. The truth that God has revealed is sufficient, but it is not exhaustive. There are many things that God has not told us. Moses wrote.

The secret things belong to the LORD our God, but the things revealed belong to us and to our children forever, that we may follow all the words of this law (Deuteronomy 29:29 NIV).

Therefore, many things about God are still unknown.

3. INFORMATION ABOUT GOD WAS SUFFICIENT AT ALL STAGES OF HUMAN HISTORY

Through the various stages of human history, God has given His people sufficient information to believe in Him. They always have had enough information to know that He existed, as well as what He required from them. Consequently, they were never left in the dark about God's existence, or how He expected them to behave.

For example, Adam and Eve were given insight into future salvation. The Book of Genesis says God gave the following words of punishment to the serpent which tempted Eve.

And I will put enmity between you and the woman, and between your offspring and hers; he will crush your head, and you will strike his heel (Genesis 3:15 NIV).

The offspring of the woman would be Jesus Christ—the Savior.

Later, we read of Cain and Abel. They were to bring an offering to the Lord.

At harvesttime Cain brought to the LORD a gift of his farm produce, while Abel brought several choice lambs from the best of his flock. The LORD accepted Abel and his offering (Genesis 4:3-4 NLT).

They realized that some payment was necessary for sin. The Lord said to them.

> You will be accepted if you respond in the right way. But
> if you refuse to respond correctly, then watch out! Sin is
> waiting to attack and destroy you, and you must subdue it
> (Genesis 4:7 NLT).

Before Jesus Christ came into the world, people were saved by looking forward to His coming. The writer to the Hebrews put it this
way.

> These all died in faith without having received the promises,
> but they saw them from a distance, greeted them, and con-
> fessed that they were foreigners and temporary residents on
> the earth (Hebrews 11:13 HCSB).

They died in faith looking forward to the promises of God. In fact, we
are told that Moses "suffered for Christ." We read in Hebrews.

> He considered the reproach of Christ greater wealth than
> the treasures of Egypt, for he was looking to the reward
> (Hebrews 11:26 ESV).

Jesus said Abraham looked forward to seeing His day. We read Him
saying the following in the Gospel of John.

> Your ancestor Abraham rejoiced as he looked forward to my
> coming. He saw it and was glad (John 8:56 NLT).

While their knowledge was limited, they were still able to act in faith
towards God's promises. They had saving faith without knowing the
exact details of Christ's death.

The key is that they trusted God's words. It is clear that their
knowledge was sufficient to act in faith toward God. Therefore, we
find that Scripture has always been adequate to meet the needs of
the people.

4. WE DO NOT NEED SOME AUTHORITY FIGURE TO INTERPRET THE BIBLE FOR US

Sometimes it is argued that Scriptures are not clear in-and-of-themselves. Thus, believers need some type of external authority to properly interpret and understand its teaching. This may come from some church, a creed, or the teaching of some church leader.

However, the facts speak otherwise. The Bible is able to be understood by the great majority of the people. Every believer should study the Scriptures for themselves. Nowhere do we find the Scripture telling believers that they should only listen to some special spiritual leader to know the truth.

5. GOD WOULD NOT GIVE US A CONFUSED REVELATION

There is something else. It is unreasonable to say, as some have done, that God would give humanity a revelation of Himself that could not be understood by the masses. To the contrary, the Bible is written in such a way that people in every age are able to understand it. Jesus made this point clear when He spoke of the nature of God the Father. He said.

> What father among you, if his son asks for a fish, will, instead of a fish, give him a snake? (Luke 11:11 HCSB).

Humanity needs a clear Word from God. God, who is compared to a loving Father, gives only good things to His children. Therefore, He would not give us a confused, or contradictory, revelation of Himself.

6. THE CREEDS AND CHURCH COUNCILS ARE INSUFFICIENT TO ESTABLISH TRUTH

Although some claim that creeds, belief statements, or the conclusions of church councils, are alternatives to Scripture, they cause more problems than they solve. Creeds and councils, no matter how orthodox, are still the pronouncements of human beings. There is no guarantee that any pronouncements they make are to be considered infallible.

The Holy Scripture alone contains all things necessary for believers. There is no need for anything to be added to them. They are sufficient.

7. JESUS ASSUMED THAT THE SCRIPTURES WERE SUFFICIENT TO ANSWER OUR QUESTIONS

The answers to the basic problems that humanity faces, such as our identity, purpose, and destiny, can be found in the pages of Scripture. Jesus acknowledged that the religious leaders of His day did indeed search the Scriptures to find answers to these questions. He said.

> You search the scriptures because you think that in them you have eternal life; and it is they that testify on my behalf. Yet you refuse to come to me to have life (John 5:39,40 NRSV).

While Jesus condemned the religious leaders for a number of their practices, He did not condemn them for searching the Scriptures.

It is interesting to note that the King James Version is different from other English translations here. It reads this as a command of Jesus—not merely a statement of what they were doing. It says.

> Search the scriptures; for in them ye think ye have eternal life: and they are they which testify of me (John 5:39 KJV).

The translation of the King James Version is possible—the Greek text can be read either as a command "search the Scriptures" or as a statement of that which they were already doing "you search the Scriptures."

8. PAUL EMPHASIZED THAT EACH BELIEVER SHOULD THOROUGHLY SEARCH THE SCRIPTURE FOR ANSWERS

Like Jesus, the Apostle Paul emphasized that people should thoroughly search the Scriptures. He wrote the following to Timothy.

> Do your best to present yourself to God as one approved by him, a worker who has no need to be ashamed, rightly explaining the word of truth (2 Timothy 2:15 NRSV).

The Scripture is the "word of truth." The reason the Scripture should be studied is because it is God's divinely inspired Word. Paul also wrote to Timothy.

> All scripture is inspired by God and is useful for teaching, for reproof, for correction, and for training in righteousness, so that everyone who belongs to God may be proficient, equipped for every good work (2 Timothy 3:16-17 NRSV).

According to Paul, those who study the Scripture can be thoroughly equipped for "every good work." Scripture is profitable for teaching, rebuking, correcting, and training in righteousness. We need nothing else to live the Christian life.

9. THE BIBLE HAS PROVED SUFFICIENT FOR US

We also should note that Scriptures have proved themselves to be sufficient. Those who read and study the Bible discover that the Scripture provides everything necessary to understand the plan of God and live a godly life. Peter wrote.

> His divine power has given us everything we need for life and godliness through our knowledge of him who called us by his own glory and goodness (2 Peter 1:3 NIV).

The psalmist equates God's blessing with obeying His Word. He wrote.

> Our Lord, you bless everyone who lives right and obeys your Law (Psalm 119:1 CEV).

This is a further indication that obedience to God consists of obeying His Word.

Therefore, the Bible itself is sufficient for human beings to know who God is, and what He wants from humanity. Consequently, nothing needs to be added to Scripture.

PRACTICAL IMPLICATIONS FROM THE DOCTRINE THE SUFFICIENCY OF SCRIPTURE

The doctrine of the sufficiency of the Bible has a number of important implications for believers. They include the following.

A. WE CAN FOCUS ON GOD'S WORD ALONE

Because the Bible contains sufficient answers to our deepest questions, we can make it our focus to find these ultimate answers. There is nowhere else that we must go.

Therefore, we do not have to spend our time finding out what various Christians leaders, or church councils, have said on a particular topic. Any conclusions they may have reached cannot be considered either as authoritative or infallible. It is only the Bible that is completely trustworthy.

Consequently, nothing outside of the Scripture has any binding authority over believers. We are not obliged to obey any command or teaching of any "Christian" group if it is not either explicitly or implicitly taught in the Bible. Guidance will come from God's Word—not from the commands or suggestions of others.

B. WE CAN EVALUATE EVERYTHING ELSE IN THE LIGHT OF SCRIPTURE

The fact that the Scriptures are sufficient does not mean that we ignore what others have written or said in the past. Indeed, it simply means that whatever they have said must be evaluated in light of Scripture. We do not disregard what others have taught on particular topics, but we do evaluate their words in light of our only trustworthy source—the Bible. While the conclusions of others may be helpful, they are not authoritative in any sense of the word.

SUMMARY TO QUESTION 24
WHAT IS THE SUFFICIENCY OF SCRIPTURE?

The sufficiency of Scripture is an important doctrine. It teaches that everything that humankind needs to know about God and ourselves has been revealed in the Bible. These truths should be studied. While the truth of Scripture is sufficient, it is not exhaustive—it does not tell us everything that we would like to know but it does inform us of everything that we *need* to know.

Consequently, believers do not need any type of external authority to understand and interpret the Scriptures—whether it may be a church, a creedal statement, or the teaching of some leader.

Indeed, it is not reasonable to think that God would give a communication to humanity that could not be understood by the masses. In fact, believers are commanded to study the Bible for themselves. God has given believers all things necessary to understand the Scriptures.

As one studies the Bible the truths about God and His plan becomes more and more clear. The Scriptures are indeed sufficient. Therefore, we should search the Bible to find out what it says about a particular matter.

There are practical results of understanding this doctrine.

First, our energy should be spent with studying the Bible to find out what it says on a particular matter. We do not have to spend endless time reading what others have said about it.

Second, while we do not completely ignore what others have said, we always evaluate their conclusions in light of our one infallible source—the Bible.

Why Should Such an Ancient Book, Like the Bible, Be Used as the Basis of Our Behavior Today?

How can the commandments of Scripture, written thousands of years ago, be binding on people today? Since the world has radically changed since the time of Jesus Christ, in what sense is the Bible still relevant? How can the Bible be considered normative in any way?

Therefore, it is fair to ask the question, "Why, then should we obey the commandments that are written in the Bible?"

A number of important points need to be made about this issue. They are as follows.

1. THE CHARACTER OF GOD HAS NOT CHANGED

While humanity may change, God does not change. The Bible says.

> Before the mountains were brought forth, or ever you had formed the earth and the world, from everlasting to everlasting you are God (Psalm 90:2 ESV).

In the Book of Malachi, we read the following.

> For I the Lord do not change; therefore you, O children of Jacob, are not consumed (Malachi 3:6 ESV).

God remains the same. It is only from Scripture that we know who He is, and what He is like. Therefore, if we want to know what God is like, we must study the Bible.

2. THE HUMAN CONDITION HAS NOT CHANGED

Human beings are the same as they have been since the time of the fall of Adam and Eve. They are still lost in sin and they still need a Savior. With all the advancements that have been made since biblical times, there is still the need for forgiveness of sin, and a personal relationship with the Creator. All the advancements of science and culture cannot even be of the slightest help in bringing a person into a right relationship with God.

3. THE WAY TO APPROACH GOD HAS NOT CHANGED

People today need to approach God in the same humble way as in the beginning. This has not changed with time. Each individual must come to the Lord in simple faith—believing in His promises. There is no other way to approach Him.

4. THE NEED FOR AN ABSOLUTE STANDARD HAS NOT CHANGED

There has always been the need for an absolute standard of right and wrong. This does not change from generation to generation. The teachings of Scripture do not change from century to century. The truths about God are still binding.

There are passages in Scripture that directly apply to all people of all times. For example, the Bible prohibits stealing. It says.

You shall not steal (Exodus 20:15 NKJV).

This passage applies to all people at all times. Stealing is always wrong. The same holds true for such things as lying, cheating, and murder.

5. ALL PORTIONS OF SCRIPTURE, NO MATTER TO WHOM THEY WERE WRITTEN, TEACH IMPORTANT PRINCIPLES

There are parts of the Bible that were addressed to individuals which dealt with specific situations. For example, Paul gave Timothy the following advice.

> No longer drink only water, but use a little wine for the sake of your stomach and your frequent ailments (1 Timothy 5:23 ESV).

On another occasion, Paul wrote to the Corinthians and said.

> All the brothers send you greetings. Greet one another with a holy kiss (1 Corinthians 16:20 ESV).

While these verses speak to specific situations, there are underlying principles that are normative and can be applied at any time. In other words, they contain truths and biblical principles that go beyond the immediate context.

6. ETERNAL TRUTHS CAN BE REVEALED IN AN ANCIENT DOCUMENT

We need to stress this final point. There is nothing illogical about claiming that eternal truths can be recorded in a document written long in the past. The claim of the church for the last two thousand years is that the teaching of the Bible is normative for all people for all time. While the biblical writers were limited to the time in which they lived, they shared things that were common to all human beings. The writings were not time-bound, though the writers lived at a distinct time in history.

While the words of Scripture are human words that were spoken and written in a particular culture at a particular time, there is nothing unreasonable about believing that they can have authority across cultures and across time. This is because the words of Scripture are the words of God. They can communicate across cultures, geography, and time. While the Bible must be interpreted in its historical setting, the message is not limited to a particular time in history.

Because the Bible is completely God's Word, it speaks eternal truth that applies to all readers, everywhere. While it was addressed to specific problems and specific needs, it does not merely apply to those who first received it. Therefore, the Scripture is just as relevant today as when it was first written—its commandments are still binding.

SUMMARY TO QUESTION 25
WHY SHOULD AN ANCIENT BOOK, LIKE THE BIBLE, BE USED AS THE BASIS OF OUR BEHAVIOR TODAY?

While some people think that the Bible is out-of-date, or irrelevant to modern humanity, this is certainly not the case. There are a number of reasons as to why the Bible is the still the most relevant book in the world.

To begin with, it is only from the Bible that we can know any specific facts about God. He does not change.

In addition, humanity is still in the same sinful condition that our first parents, Adam and Eve, found themselves in. Furthermore, the way in which a person approaches God has not changed through time.

The Bible also provides a necessary absolute standard of right and wrong. All of Scripture, no matter to whom it was originally addressed, contains important principles for us today.

For these reasons the Bible remains the most relevant book for humanity in our present day.

About the Author

Don Stewart is a graduate of Biola University and Talbot Theological Seminary (with the highest honors).

Don is a best-selling and award-winning author having authored, or co-authored, over seventy books. This includes the best-selling *Answers to Tough Questions*, with Josh McDowell, as well as the award-winning book *Family Handbook of Christian Knowledge: The Bible*. His various writings have been translated into over thirty different languages and have sold over a million copies.

Don has traveled around the world proclaiming and defending the historic Christian faith. He has also taught both Hebrew and Greek at the undergraduate level and Greek at the graduate level.

Made in the USA
Columbia, SC
01 July 2021